SHOOT UP TO THE TOEIC® TEST LISTENING

Kinseido Publishing Co., Ltd.
3-21 Kanda Jimbo-cho, Chiyoda-ku,
Tokyo 101-0051, Japan

First published 2024 by Kinseido Publishing Co., Ltd.

Cover design Takayuki Minegishi
Text design　C-leps Co., Ltd.

音声ファイル無料ダウンロード

https://www.kinsei-do.co.jp/download/4208

この教科書で DL 00 の表示がある箇所の音声は、上記 URL または QR コードにて無料でダウンロードできます。自習用音声としてご活用ください。

- ▶ PC からのダウンロードをお勧めします。スマートフォンなどでダウンロードされる場合は、**ダウンロード前に「解凍アプリ」をインストール**してください。
- ▶ URL は、**検索ボックスではなくアドレスバー(URL 表示覧)**に入力してください。
- ▶ お使いのネットワーク環境によっては、ダウンロードできない場合があります。

CD 00　左記の表示がある箇所の音声は、教室用 CD（Class Audio CD）に収録されています。

はしがき

TOEIC を学ぶ皆さんへ

TOEIC は、今や大学生や社会人の必須テストです。

日本や韓国を中心に世界 160 カ国で実施され、国内の受験者は年間 200 万人を超えました。英語コミュニケーション力の認定テストとして、ビジネスの現場や日常生活において、どの程度のコミュニケーション力があるかを測定するのがTOEIC です。最も受験者の多いTOEIC® Listening & Reading Testの「公開テスト」と「団体テスト（IP）」では、リスニング（Part 1 ～ 4）とリーディング（Part 5 ～ 7）が各100問（計200問）出題されます。他に、TOEIC® Speaking & Writing TestsやTOEIC® Speaking Test、TOEIC Bridge®（初級者向け）があります。

本書は、TOEIC の「リスニング」にターゲットを絞っています。2015年度に発行した前書、*STRIKE UP THE TOEIC® TEST LISTENING* を新形式のテストに対応させ、改訂しました。リスニング力を向上させて、ハイスコアを目指しましょう。

本書の構成

本書は全 24 のUNIT で構成されています。各UNIT では、TOEIC 頻出のテーマを厳選しました。毎回、Part 1 ～ 4 までのリスニングセクションをまるごと学習する構成になっています。

各 Part 学習 STEP

パターンとテクニックを身につけよう

TOEIC の「リスニング」では、「耳」を鍛えることが大事です。加えて、Part 3 & 4 では、設問と選択肢を読む「リーディング」力も問われます。その能力向上には、テストパターンを把握し、効率良く解答するテクニックが不可欠です。結果、英語力が上がれば言うことなしですね。本書を活用して、TOEIC のスコアアップを目指してください。

塚田幸光

SHOOT UP TO THE TOEIC® TEST LISTENING Contents

TOEIC の構成

Listening Section（100 問）　解答時間約 45 分

Part 1 写真描写問題（6 問） →詳しい説明や攻略法は 6 ページ参照	1 枚の写真に関する短い 4 つの英文（選択肢）が放送されます。4 つのうち、写真を最も的確に描写しているものを選びます。選択肢は印刷されていません。
Part 2 応答問題（25 問） →詳しい説明や攻略法は 7 ページ参照	1 つの問いかけ（質問文）に対し、3 つの応答（選択肢）が放送されます。設問に対して最もふさわしい応答を選びます。問いかけも応答も印刷されていません。
Part 3 会話問題（39 問） →詳しい説明や攻略法は 8 ページ参照	2 人、または 3 人の人物による会話が放送されます。会話を聞いて、問題用紙に印刷された設問と選択肢を読み、その中から最も適当なものを選びます。各会話には設問が 3 つずつあります。また、会話と問題用紙に印刷された図表を関連づけて答える問題も出題されます。
Part 4 説明文問題（30 問） →詳しい説明や攻略法は 9 ページ参照	アナウンスなどの説明文が放送されます。各説明文を聞いて、問題用紙に印刷された設問と選択肢を読み、その中から最も適当なものを選びます。各説明文には設問が 3 つずつあります。また、説明文と問題用紙に印刷された図表を関連づけて答える問題も出題されます。

Reading Section（100 問）　解答時間 75 分

Part 5 短文穴埋め問題（30 問） →詳しい説明や攻略法は 10 ページ参照	不完全な短文の空所を補う語句として、最も適当なものを 4 つの選択肢の中から選び、文章を完成させます。
Part 6 長文穴埋め問題（16 問） →詳しい説明や攻略法は 11 ページ参照	メールなどの不完全な長文の空所を補う語句や文を、4 つの選択肢の中から選びます。品詞問題、文法問題、語彙問題、そして文選択問題の 4 パターンがあります。
Part 7 読解問題（54 問） →詳しい説明や攻略法は 12 ページ参照	メールや社内メモ、広告などの長文とそれに関する各設問を読み、4 つの選択肢の中から最も適当なものを選びます。1 つの文章を読んで問いに答えるシングル・パッセージは 10 セット（29 問）、ダブル・パッセージは 2 セット（10 問）、トリプル・パッセージは 3 セット（15 問）出題されます。

TOEIC パート別
攻略ポイント

TOEIC では、限られた時間内で 200 問という多くの問題を解く必要があります。高いスコアを取るには、ただやみくもに問題を解くのではなく、「戦略」を考えて挑むことが不可欠です。ここでは、パートそれぞれの攻略ポイントを紹介します。試験直前などに、ここをザッと見ておくことをお勧めします。なお、本書では、リスニングセクション（Part 1 ～ Part 4）を扱います。

Part 1 の攻略ポイント

形式

問題数：6 問

選択肢数：4 つ

所要時間：約 4 分 30 秒（問題 1 問につき約 45 秒）

目標解答時間：1 問＝約 5 秒

注意点：4 つの英文（選択肢）は、テスト用紙に印刷されていません

攻略 STEP

STEP ①
写真を
見る
「目立つもの」を
チェック！
STEP ②
放送を
聞く
ポイントを
待ち伏せよう！
STEP ③
TOEIC 的
トリックに注意
出題パターンを
意識して！

STEP ①…写真を見る

Part 1 の写真では、**「人物」と「風景」の2パターン**が出ます。細かい事柄ではなく、一番**「目立つもの（人）」をチェック**します。

STEP ②…放送を聞く

写真のポイントを把握して、ポイントとなる音を待ち伏せしましょう。チェック・ポイントは以下です。

＜人物写真＞	＜風景写真＞
1．人数・性別	1．場所
2．特徴（外見・服装）	2．物（目立つモノ）
3．動作（何をしているか）	3．状態・位置（カタチを見る）

STEP ③…TOEIC 的トリックに注意

1．似ている音（coffee / copy や car / cart などの似ている音に注意！）

2．言い換え（bus でなく vehicle という抽象的な語への言い換えに注意！）

3．カタチを見抜く（side by side などの「位置・状態」フレーズが頻出！）

Part 2 の攻略ポイント

形式

問題数：25 問
選択肢数：3 つ
所要時間：約 8 分（問題 1 問につき約 19 秒）
目標解答時間：1 問＝約 5 秒
注意点：問いかけ・応答は、テスト用紙に印刷されていません

攻略 STEP

STEP ①
疑問詞を
聞く
質問文の 5W1H
を聞く！
STEP ②
パターンを
予測する
質問文と応答の
パターンをチェック！
STEP ③
テクニックを
使う
音テクニックが
生命線！

STEP ①…疑問詞を聞く

Part 2 では、**最初の 1 語の聞き取りが最大のポイント**です。**5W1H 疑問詞**（Who, What, When, Where, Why, How）さえわかれば、半分以上が解けます。まずは、「疑問詞」を聞くことから始めましょう。

STEP ②…パターンを予測する

Part 2 は、5W1H 疑問文の他に**7つの質問文パターン**があります。①付加疑問文（..., isn't it?）、②ふつうの疑問文（Do you ...?）、③否定疑問文（Don't you ...?）、④提案・勧誘（Why don't you ...?）、⑤依頼文（Will you ...?）、⑥選択疑問文（A or B?）、⑦平叙文（？マークがないふつうの文）です。それぞれにパターンがあるので、本編で確認しましょう。

STEP ③…テクニックを使う

音のテクニックは、主に 2 つ。Part 2 の定番なのでマスターしましょう。

1．音の反復は×

質問文で聞こえた単語が、応答文でも聞こえたら、その選択肢は×。

2．誤連想も×

聞こえた音から、関連する単語を（勝手に）連想してはダメ。

Part 3 の攻略ポイント

形式

問題数：39 問（会話 13 セット、各会話に設問が 3 つ）
選択肢数：4 つ
所要時間：約 18 分（「会話＋設問」セット 1 つが約 1 分 20 秒）
目標解答時間：1 設問＝約 8 秒、図表問題＝約 12 秒
注意点：設問と選択肢はテスト用紙に印刷されています

攻略 STEP

STEP ①
設問を
先読みする
「全体」と「部分」
の設問を見抜く
STEP ②
設問パターンを
チェック！
会話のポイントを
予測する
STEP ③
ポイントを
待ち伏せる
ポイントを待ち伏
せてリスニング！

STEP ①…設問を先読みする

設問には 2 パターンあります。会話文の目的や状況、場所などを問う「主題」に関する設問（＝**「全体」を問う設問**）と、会話文の細部を問う設問（＝**「部分」を問う設問**）です。設問をパッと見て「全体」か「部分」かをチェックします。

STEP ②…設問パターンをチェック！

「全体」を問う設問は、**会話の冒頭**に解答のヒントがあります。一方、「部分」を問う設問では、**設問の「主語」**と**名詞「キーワード」**をチェックしましょう。例えば、What will the man do by this afternoon?（男性は今日の午後までに何をしますか）であれば、主語を見れば男女どちらの会話にヒントがあるかが明白ですし、キーワードはリスニングの耳印になります。また、図表問題では、選択肢にない図表中の情報が解答のヒントになります。

STEP ③…ポイントを待ち伏せる

放送を聞く前に、①と②の設問ポイントをチェックします。このチェックがあれば、設問のポイントを待ち伏せた上でのリスニングができるはずです。

Part 4 の攻略ポイント

形式

問題数：30 問（説明文 10 セット、各説明文に設問が 3 つ）
選択肢数：4 つ
所要時間：約 15 分（「説明文＋設問」セット 1 つが約 1 分 30 秒）
目標解答時間：1 設問＝8 秒、図表問題＝12 秒
注意点：設問と選択肢はテスト用紙に印刷されています

攻略 STEP

STEP ①…設問を先読みする

Part 3 と同じく、まず「全体」と「部分」の設問をチェックします。「全体」ならば、冒頭に集中して、主題をつかめば OK。「部分」はキーワードをチェックして、ポイントを待ち伏せします。

STEP ②…ジャンルをチェック！

Part 4 では、**「スピーチ」**、**「アナウンス」**、**「ニュース」**、**「広告」**、**「ツアーガイド」**、**「電話メッセージ」**など、説明文のジャンルが決まっています。例えば、電話メッセージでは、旅行代理店から客への旅程確認、病院から患者への予約確認など、内容はパターン化されています。

STEP ③…定番問題を得点源に！

「部分」を問う設問には、得点源になる定番問題があります。What does the speaker ask ～？（話し手は何を求めていますか）のような「依頼問題」では、本文の Could you ～？がヒントです。また、What does the speaker say he will do next?（話し手は次に何をすると言っていますか）のような「do next 問題」では、本文の I'll ～がポイントになります。定番問題の解答パターンを知ることは、スコアアップの鍵になります。

Part 5 の攻略ポイント

形式

問題数：30 問
選択肢数：4 つ
目標解答時間：1 問＝約 30 秒（全体で 20 分以内）

攻略 STEP

STEP ①…選択肢を見る

Part 5 では、まず選択肢を見ます。以下のパターンから問題を把握します。

1．選択肢の品詞がバラバラな場合→「品詞問題」
2．選択肢の品詞に共通点がある場合→「文法問題」もしくは「語彙問題」

STEP ②…空所の前後を見る

空所の前後を見て、解答のヒントを探します。意味を取るのではなく、カタチを見ることが大事！

1．「品詞問題」→空所の品詞を見抜けば OK
2．「文法問題」→空所の前後に「文法ヒント」を探す
　例えば、recently があるときは、空所は過去形か現在完了形。
3．「語彙問題」→空所の前後に「フレーズのカップリング」を探す
　例えば、office (supplies) や (issue) a warning といった組み合わせ。

STEP ③…「接続詞」問題に注意！

Part 5 では、①②のポイントで「意味ではなくカタチから解く」のが大事です。ただし例外はいくつかあります。その代表格が「接続詞」問題。文構造と意味の両方から解く必要があります。

Part 6 の攻略ポイント

形式

問題数：16 問（文書 4 セット）
選択肢数：4 つ
目標解答時間：1 文書（4 問）＝ 2 分 30 秒以内（4 セットで 10 分）

攻略 STEP

STEP ①…ジャンルをチェック！

Part 6 では、Part 7 同様、メールや広告などのビジネス文書が出題されます。ジャンルをチェックすることで、文書の展開が予測できます。例えば「広告」ならば、〈①商品・サービス案内⇒②内容説明⇒③追加情報〉という流れですね。

STEP ②…選択肢を見る！

Part 6 では、品詞問題は即答しましょう。ですが、「文法問題」（時制、接続副詞、代名詞）、「語彙問題」、「文選択問題」は、難関の文脈問題です。空所前後だけで解けない問題が増えているのも近年の特徴です。

STEP ③…全文をスパッと読みながら解く！

品詞問題を即答したら、文書全体をザッと読みながら文脈問題を解きましょう。特に「文選択問題」は、選択肢も長い難問です。選択肢の名詞をヒントに、文書を読まねばなりません。

Part 7 の攻略ポイント

形式

問題数：54 問
シングル・パッセージ：文書 10、設問数 29 問
ダブル・パッセージ：文書 2 セット、設問数 10 問
トリプル・パッセージ：文書 3 セット、設問数 15 問
目標解答時間：1 問 1 分（全体で 55 分以内）

攻略 STEP

STEP ①
ジャンルを
チェック！
文書ジャンルを
把握しよう
STEP ②
設問を
チェック！
「全体」「部分」「難」
を見抜く！
STEP ③
サーチ＆
ファインド！
設問の該当箇所を
文書に探す

STEP ①…ジャンルをチェック！

Part 7 では、特定のジャンルの文書が出題されます。その内容も一定なので、パターンを把握しておくと有利です。ジャンルには **「メール」**、**「手紙」**、**「広告」**、**「通知」**、**「記事」**、**「プレスリリース」**、**「フォーム」**、**「説明書」** などがあります。

STEP ②…設問をチェック！

Part 3 & 4 と同じく、設問にはパターンがあります。「全体」を問う設問、「部分」を問う設問、「難」設問をチェックしましょう。特に「難」設問は、3 つの「i」を含む設問 (indicate, imply, infer) に加え、本文と選択肢の比較検討が必要な「NOT を含む設問」(NOT 問題) が要注意です。また、ダブル・パッセージ問題では 2 つの文書、トリプル・パッセージ問題では 3 つの文書からヒントを拾う「クロス問題」も出題されます。

STEP ③…サーチ＆ファインド！

Part 7 の標準解答時間は、1 問 1 分です。文章をゆっくり読んでいる時間はありません。設問の該当箇所をサーチ＆ファインドして、即答しましょう。

Unit 1

Daily Life

TOEIC ではビジネスだけでなく、日常生活に関するトピックも多く出題されます。電話表現や道案内のやりとりを中心に基本事項をチェックしましょう。

Part 1 Photographs

DL 002, 003 CD1-02 CD1-03

Look at the picture and choose the statement that best describes what you see.

1. (A) (B) (C) (D)

「動作」を聞こう！
動詞に耳を澄まして！

2. (A) (B) (C) (D)

人物が何をしているか
をチェック！

Part 2 Question-Response

DL 004 ~007 CD1-04 ~ CD1-07

Choose the best response to each question or statement.

3. (A) (B) (C)

4. (A) (B) (C)

5. (A) (B) (C)

6. (A) (B) (C)

まず、「疑問詞」を聞こう！5W1H に集中！

Part 3 Short Conversations

Listen to a short conversation, and choose the best answer to each question.

7. What is the reason the man is calling?

マイナスワード、本文のUnfortunatelyをキャッチしよう！

(A) He wants to express his satisfaction.
(B) The invoice amount is incorrect.
(C) Something was broken during the visit.
(D) He received someone else's bill.

8. What does the man mean when he says, "I handled the waste by myself"?

文脈とターゲット文をつなげよう！

(A) The invoice included a disposal fee.
(B) The customer was charged an extension fee.
(C) The movers disposed of the garbage.
(D) He wanted them to take care of his trash.

9. What does the woman offer to do?

offerを見たら、本文のI willを待て！

(A) Return a telephone call
(B) Revise the invoice
(C) Exchange contact information
(D) Make a checklist

Part 4 Short Talks

Listen to a short talk, and choose the best answer to each question.

10. What kind of company is GP Union Electric?

> 「どんな会社」→ 選択肢4つを「タテ読み」！

(A) Social services

(B) A labor union

(C) A repair company

(D) An appliance store

11. Why is Travis Samuel calling?

(A) To ask for a monetary donation

(B) To verify customer satisfaction

(C) To publicize a new company service

(D) To offer a free upgrade coupon

> 電話した理由は、I'm calling の後を聞く！

12. According to the speaker, how can the listener report problems?

> 〈How → By〉のパターンは定番！説明文の後半にヒント！

(A) By writing a letter

(B) By visiting the company

(C) By sending back the questionnaire

(D) By participating in a survey

Unit 2

Restaurant

レストランでは、テーブルの予約、キャンセル、注文のやりとりが定番です。シチュエーションをイメージして、関連表現を覚えましょう。

Part 1 Photographs

Look at the picture and choose the statement that best describes what you see.

1. (A)　(B)　(C)　(D)

人物２人の「状態」に注目！

2. (A)　(B)　(C)　(D)

「空席」は何て言う？
定番ワードをキャッチ！

Part 2 Question-Response

DL 014 ~ 017 CD1-20 ~ CD1-23

Choose the best response to each question or statement.

3. (A) (B) (C)
4. (A) (B) (C)
5. (A) (B) (C)
6. (A) (B) (C)

トリッキーな応答に注意しよう

Part 3 Short Conversations

Listen to a short conversation, and choose the best answer to each question.

7. Why is the woman calling?

電話の「理由」は、I'm calling が「耳印」！

(A) To order a set menu
(B) To cancel an event
(C) To book a flight
(D) To find a place for a party

8. What does the man say about dates?

「日付」はくせ者！ダミー日付に惑わされるな！

(A) None are available.
(B) There are two days to choose from.
(C) The 15th is reserved.
(D) Dates are all set.

9. What does the woman decide to do?

セオリー通り「主語」をチェック！

(A) Call again in December
(B) Have a 4-hour party
(C) Make a tentative reservation
(D) Pay a cancellation charge

Part 4 Short Talks

DL 020, 021 CD1-29 ~ CD1-32

Listen to a short talk, and choose the best answer to each question.

10. What does the shopping mall plan to hold for four days?

設問のキーワードを待ち伏せよう！

(A) A flower festival
(B) A sculpture exhibition
(C) A food festival
(D) A jazz concert

11. According to the speaker, what can't the customers do during the festival for the restaurant?

「客ができないこと」は何？
→ not を含む注意点を聞こう！

(A) Order specialties of the restaurant
(B) Apply for the events held in the restaurant
(C) Drive to the restaurant
(D) Make reservations directly

12. Look at the graphic. On which day will the famous flower artist's events take place?

Event Schedule from 5 p.m. to 8 p.m. at the Oceanfront Restaurant	
Thursday	Joe Carter's Gardeners Lecture and Talk Show
Friday	The FLOWERS Jazz Concert
Saturday	Marshal Crane Live Performance
Sunday	Flower Shop Award Ceremony

何のイベントかをキャッチ！

(A) Thursday
(B) Friday
(C) Saturday
(D) Sunday

Unit 3 Party

TOEIC は大のパーティ好き。会社主催のオフィスパーティに加え、歓迎会や送別会もよく出ます。パーティに関するやりとりに慣れましょう。

Part 1 Photographs

DL 022, 023　CD1-33　CD1-34

Look at the picture and choose the statement that best describes what you see.

1. (A)　(B)　(C)　(D)

人物の「特徴」をチェック！
外見・服装は？

2. (A)　(B)　(C)　(D)

風景写真では
「目立つもの」を見よう！

Part 2 Question-Response

DL 024～027　CD1-35 ～ CD1-38

Choose the best response to each question or statement.

3. (A)　(B)　(C)
4. (A)　(B)　(C)
5. (A)　(B)　(C)
6. (A)　(B)　(C)

「音の反復」は不正解！
音テクをマスターして！

Part 3 Short Conversations

DL 028, 029 CD1-39 ~ CD1-43

Listen to a short conversation, and choose the best answer to each question.

7. Where most likely are the speakers?

(A) On a golf course (B) At a company (C) On a mountain (D) At a party

話し手の「場所」を問う定番！
冒頭の数秒にヒント！

8. Who is Gordon?

(A) A school friend (B) An old client (C) An office superior (D) A new worker

Who 設問では、「職業」「職種」が問われる！

9. What is being planned?

(A) A golf trip (B) An overseas visit (C) A farewell party (D) A mountain trek

TOEIC はイベント好き！

Part 4 Short Talks

DL 030, 031 CD1-44 ~ CD1-47

Listen to a short talk, and choose the best answer to each question.

10. How long has Jennifer Howell been working for Central Electric?

(A) For two years (B) For three years (C) For five years (D) For fifteen years

「勤務年数」はよく出る！
冒頭の数字をキャッチ！

11. What does Jennifer Howell do now?

now がポイント！彼女の今の役職は？

(A) She has retired from Central Electric.
(B) She is the General Manager at the Windsor branch.
(C) She works in the customer service department.
(D) She is the head of all the business in part of the country.

12. What will the speaker most likely do next?

do next を見たら、
本文の一番最後にヒント！

(A) Ask Jennifer Howell to make a speech
(B) Make a phone call to General Manager
(C) Work to restore power to all customers
(D) Enjoy some food and beverages

Unit 4

Airport

空港は頻出シチュエーション。送迎トピックに加え、様々なトラブル・トピックに注意しましょう。なかでも、飛行機の「遅延」は毎回出ます。

Part 1 Photographs

DL 032, 033 

Look at the picture and choose the statement that best describes what you see.

1. (A) (B) (C) (D)

push と pull、混同してはダメ！

2. (A) (B) (C) (D)

選択肢の「主語」の違いに気をつけて！

Part 2 Question-Response

DL 034 ~037 

~ 

Choose the best response to each question or statement.

3. (A) (B) (C)
4. (A) (B) (C)
5. (A) (B) (C)
6. (A) (B) (C)

「提案・勧誘」は定番フレーズを暗記しよう

Part 3 Short Conversations

DL 038, 039 CD1-54 ~ CD1-58

Listen to a short conversation, and choose the best answer to each question.

7. Who most likely is the woman?

(A) A flight attendant (C) A travel agent

(B) An airline staff (D) A secretary

定番の Who 設問！
冒頭からシチュエーションを
把握すれば簡単！

8. When will the man arrive?

When 設問は、意外と「難」！

(A) At 2:00 p.m. (C) At 6:00 p.m.

(B) At 4:00 p.m. (D) At 7:00 p.m.

選択肢の「名詞キーワード」
をチェック！これを耳印に
して、本文を聞こう！

9. Why does the man prefer the flight with the layover?

(A) He will arrive earlier. (C) He wants to visit Chicago.

(B) He hates bad weather. (D) He has to attend the meeting.

Part 4 Short Talks

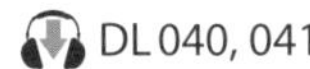

~
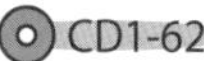

Listen to a short talk, and choose the best answer to each question.

10. Where is this announcement being made?

アナウンスの「場所」もよく出る！
冒頭の数秒に集中！

(A) At a hotel (C) At a station

(B) At an airport (D) At a theater

11. Why is the flight canceled?

フライトキャンセルは、
本文の due to を待て！

(A) Some passengers have to stay at hotels.

(B) Some coupons have been lost.

(C) An airplane needs to be fixed.

(D) There are too many customers.

12. What are listeners asked to do?

ask 問題→本文の please 以下にヒント！

(A) Remain where they are

(B) Get additional information from staff

(C) Give out free vouchers

(D) Find hotels by themselves

Unit 5

Hotel

ホテルも頻出のシチュエーションです。フロントでの予約、キャンセル、支払いに加え、クリーニングなどのルームサービスやトラブルもよく出ます。

Part 1 Photographs

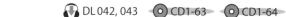

DL 042, 043　CD1-63　CD1-64

Look at the picture and choose the statement that best describes what you see.

1. (A)　(B)　(C)　(D)

2. (A)　(B)　(C)　(D)

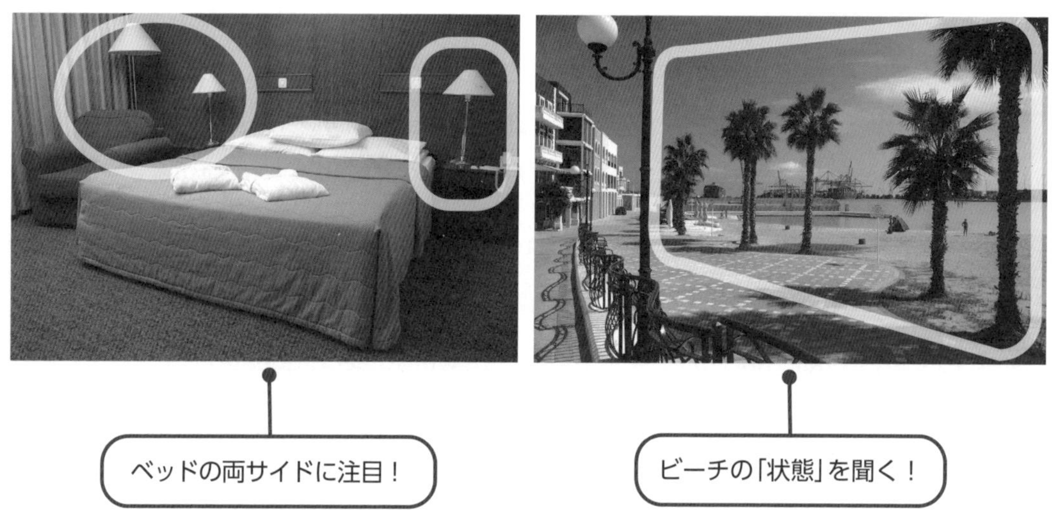

ベッドの両サイドに注目！
ビーチの「状態」を聞く！

Part 2 Question-Response

DL 044～047　CD1-65 ～ CD1-68

Choose the best response to each question or statement.

3. (A)　(B)　(C)
4. (A)　(B)　(C)
5. (A)　(B)　(C)
6. (A)　(B)　(C)

「選択疑問文」は
or のキャッチが大事！

Part 3 Short Conversations

DL 048, 049 CD1-69 ～ CD1-73

Listen to a short conversation, and choose the best answer to each question.

7. Where is the conversation taking place?
   (A) At a travel agency
   (B) At an international airport
   (C) At a shopping center
   (D) At a resort hotel

会話の「場所」は冒頭を聞こう！

8. What is wrong with Room 502?
   (A) It doesn't have a beach view.
   (B) There is no parking space.
   (C) The balcony is too big.
   (D) It's too far to the beach.

何のトラブルかをつかもう！

9. What does the woman offer to do?
   (A) Arrange a new table
   (B) Provide another room
   (C) Give a refund
   (D) Check the website

offer 問題→本文 I'll を待ちぶせ！

Part 4 Short Talks

DL 050, 051 CD1-74 ～ CD1-77

Listen to a short talk, and choose the best answer to each question.

10. Who most likely is the listener of this message?
   (A) A current guest
   (B) A cleaning person
   (C) A secretary
   (D) A board director

電話メッセージの「聞き手」は誰？冒頭からイメージする！

11. What type of room does Mr. Collins usually have?
   (A) One with a view of the pool
   (B) One on the 8th floor
   (C) One close to the lobby
   (D) One with easy access to the rooftop pool

いつも泊まっている部屋は？ usually に注目しよう

12. What does the speaker want the listener to do?
   (A) Cancel the visit
   (B) Telephone back soon
   (C) Book the room earlier
   (D) Change the direction

want 問題は、本文 Please / Would you ～？にヒント！

Unit 6

Traffic

交通トピックは、道路の状況把握がカギとなります。駐車、渋滞、工事など、様々なケースに対応しなければなりません。関連表現をしっかり覚えましょう。

Part 1 Photographs

DL 052, 053 CD1-78 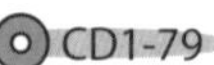

Look at the picture and choose the statement that best describes what you see.

1. (A) (B) (C) (D)

「一列に駐車」は何て言う？

2. (A) (B) (C) (D)

「同じ方向」
もよく出る！

Part 2 Question-Response

DL 054～057  ～ 

Choose the best response to each question or statement.

3. (A) (B) (C)
4. (A) (B) (C)
5. (A) (B) (C)
6. (A) (B) (C)

「否定疑問文」では、Didn't you
= Did you のように考える

Part 3 Short Conversations

DL 058, 059 CD1-84 ~ CD1-88

Listen to a short conversation, and choose the best answer to each question.

7. What is the woman's problem?

「トラブル」をキャッチ！

(A) There are no tickets left.
(B) The train has departed.
(C) She bought the wrong ticket.
(D) The machine is out of order.

8. When will the woman probably be returning?

選択肢の「言い換え」に注意！

(A) On the same day
(B) The day after tomorrow
(C) In less than a week
(D) After several weeks

will do = will do next 問題は
会話の最後にヒント！

9. What does the man say he will do?

(A) Give her a one-way ticket
(B) Charge more money
(C) Offer an open ticket
(D) Fix the machine

Part 4 Short Talks

DL 060, 061 

Listen to a short talk, and choose the best answer to each question.

10. Where does this announcement most likely take place?

アナウンスの「場所」
→冒頭に集中！

(A) In an airport
(B) In a bus station
(C) In a subway car
(D) In a traffic report

11. What does the speaker suggest people going to City Central do to avoid delays?

提案をキャッチしよう！

(A) Wait until they stop
(B) Get off and walk
(C) Use the Blue Line
(D) Avoid the Yellow Line

12. Why is the public transportation clean in Laurelton?

地名＝名詞キーワード！
キーワードを待ち伏せ！

(A) Eating and drinking is not allowed.
(B) Users throw away refuse properly.
(C) Sanitation workers have been recently hired.
(D) The station staff collects rubbish.

Unit 7

Tour & Event

旅行やイベント関連のトピックはおなじみですね。チケットの予約・キャンセル、ツアーガイドによる案内、ホテルを会場とするイベントなどが頻出です。

Part 1 Photographs

Look at the picture and choose the statement that best describes what you see.

1. (A) (B) (C) (D)

2. (A) (B) (C) (D)

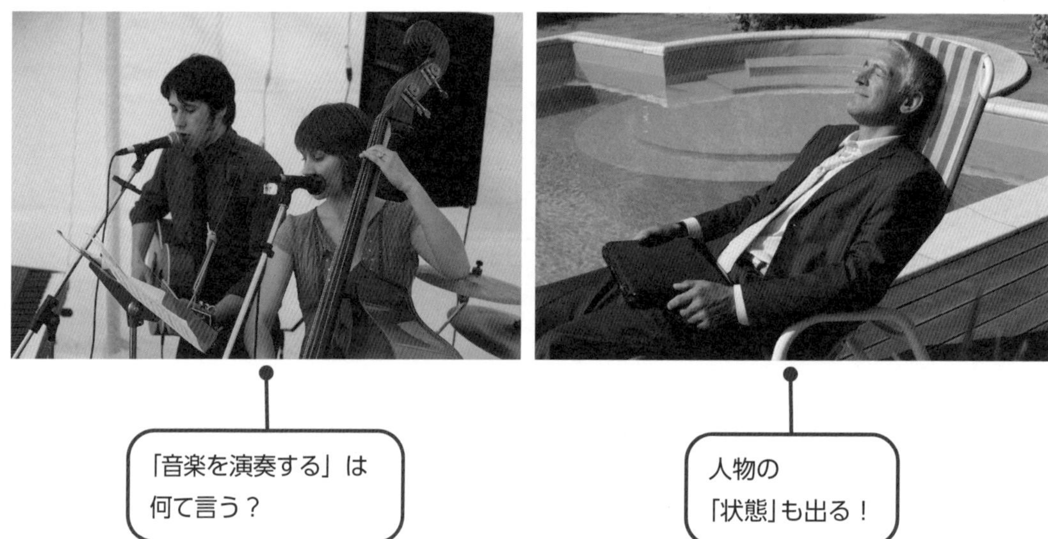

「音楽を演奏する」は何て言う？

人物の「状態」も出る！

Part 2 Question-Response

DL 064 ~067 CD2-04 ~ 

Choose the best response to each question or statement.

3. (A) (B) (C)
4. (A) (B) (C)
5. (A) (B) (C)
6. (A) (B) (C)

「付加疑問文」の文尾(aren't you? など) は無視しよう

Part 3 Short Conversations

DL 068, 069 CD2-08 ~ CD2-15

Listen to a short conversation, and choose the best answer to each question.

7. Where most likely are the speakers?

会話の場所をキャッチ！

(A) In the customer's room

(B) In a snack bar

(C) At a tour desk

(D) At a tour venue

8. Why is it a problem to set out and then turn back if it starts to rain?

トラブル問題では
マイナスワードが重要！

(A) Rough roads and hills are dangerous in the rain.

(B) Horses do not like to walk in the rain.

(C) The van might break down in the rain.

(D) They will not be able to enjoy the beautiful scenery.

9. Which alternative selection does the man probably make?

選択肢のタテ読みで、「代替案」を予測！

(A) Horseback riding

(B) Making ceramics

(C) Sports climbing

(D) Touring art galleries

Part 4 Short Talks

DL 070, 071 CD2-16 ~ CD2-19

Listen to a short talk, and choose the best answer to each question.

10. What is the purpose of the radio announcement?

アナウンスの「目的」は
冒頭に集中！

(A) To give a weather forecast
(B) To announce changes in the park schedule
(C) To talk about the most popular event in the city
(D) To ask for volunteers to set up booths and stalls

11. Where is the Pumpkin Parade held every year?

パレードの「場所」は、
本文 held in のあとを聞こう！

(A) In Pumpkin Park
(B) In City Park
(C) In Jefferson Park
(D) In Middleton Park

12. According to the speaker, what will happen this month?

キーワードをチェック！

(A) A performance will take place.
(B) The park will be decorated.
(C) Booths and stalls will be removed.
(D) Volunteers will clean the event site.

Unit 8

Shopping

日常生活のなかでもショッピングは定番トピックです。ショッピングのお誘いや商品をめぐるやりとりなど、出題ポイントは決まっています。

Part 1 Photographs

DL 072, 073

CD2-20

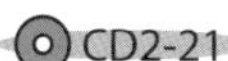

CD2-21

Look at the picture and choose the statement that best describes what you see.

1. (A) (B) (C) (D)

「一列に陳列」
は何て言う？

2. (A) (B) (C) (D)

商品の「展示」
は必ず出る！

Part 2 Question-Response

DL 074 ~ 077 CD2-22 ~ CD2-25

Choose the best response to each question or statement.

3. (A) (B) (C)
4. (A) (B) (C)
5. (A) (B) (C)
6. (A) (B) (C)

「提案・勧誘」の応答はくせ者が多い！

Part 3 Short Conversations

DL 078, 079 CD 2-26 ~ CD2-30

Listen to a short conversation, and choose the best answer to each question.

7. Where are the two speakers?

会話の「場所」！セオリー通り、冒頭を聞こう！

(A) At a design office
(B) At an accessory boutique
(C) At a grocery store
(D) At a supply warehouse

8. What does the woman say about her mother?

mother は待ち伏せキーワード！

(A) Her favorite color is beige.
(B) Her birthday was last week.
(C) She loves a certain designer.
(D) She knows the artist personally.

9. What will the man probably do next?

do next を見たら、本文 I'll ~ のあとにヒント！

(A) Telephone to check the stock
(B) Talk to the woman's mother
(C) Order a beige product
(D) Contact the designer directly

Part 4 Short Talks

Listen to a short talk, and choose the best answer to each question.

10. What did the speaker think about the shop?

店の印象は冒頭でつかむ！

(A) She was exhausted by the various processes and advice.

(B) She was impressed by the careful attention and advice.

(C) She was amazed at how everything was handmade.

(D) She was surprised at how they had finished so quickly.

11. Look at the graphic. Which pattern does the speaker want to change her order to?

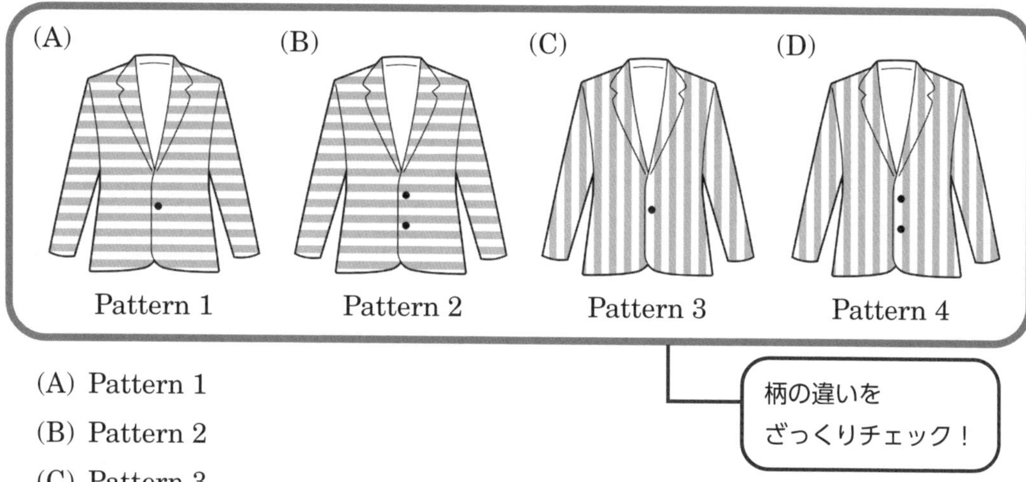

柄の違いを
ざっくりチェック！

(A) Pattern 1

(B) Pattern 2

(C) Pattern 3

(D) Pattern 4

12. Why does the speaker want to change her order this week?

設問の情報を最大限に活かそう！

(A) To get the jacket as soon as possible

(B) To avoid paying additional money

(C) To receive a previously unavailable discount

(D) To be able to get it by the date promised

Unit 9

Service

TOEIC ではサービス業務が頻出です。店頭の会話、セール案内、ラジオ広告等々。クレームのトピックが多いのも特徴です。

Part 1 Photographs

DL 082, 083　CD2-35　CD2-36

Look at the picture and choose the statement that best describes what you see.

1. (A)　(B)　(C)　(D)

「動作」は必ずチェック！

2. (A)　(B)　(C)　(D)

「手を伸ばす」は頻出！

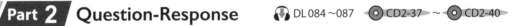

Part 2 Question-Response

DL 084 ~087　CD2-37 ~ CD2-40

Choose the best response to each question or statement.

3. (A)　(B)　(C)
4. (A)　(B)　(C)
5. (A)　(B)　(C)
6. (A)　(B)　(C)

選択疑問文の応答は、イレギュラーが多い！

Part 3 Short Conversations

DL 088, 089 CD2-41 ~ CD2-45

Listen to a short conversation, and choose the best answer to each question.

7. What is the purpose of the call?

電話の「目的」！
セオリー通り、冒頭を聞こう！

(A) To check some local news
(B) To arrange a safety check
(C) To book a job interview
(D) To rent a room

8. When is the woman available?

available はどういう意味？

(A) Monday to Friday
(B) Sunday afternoon
(C) Saturday morning
(D) Weekdays only

9. How long will the visit take?

「期間」→ 選択肢の
言い換えに注意

(A) A few minutes
(B) Ten minutes
(C) Thirty minutes
(D) About an hour

Part 4 Short Talks

DL 090, 091 CD1-46 ~ CD1-49

Listen to a short talk, and choose the best answer to each question.

10. What is the purpose of the advertisement?

広告の「目的」！
冒頭にヒント！

(A) To publicize new luxury seats
(B) To list holiday closing times
(C) To announce the winner of a contest
(D) To talk about a new bus route campaign

11. What kind of services are available on Apple Bus?

どんなサービス？
→ 先に選択肢を見る

(A) TV
(B) Full reclining seats
(C) Free drink bar
(D) Internet access

12. When does the discount offer end?

「割引期間」はよく出る！

(A) In fifty days
(B) In half an hour
(C) In four weeks
(D) In ten days

Unit 10

Health

健康関連のトピックは、意外な盲点かもしれません。病院の予約・キャンセルに加え、オフィスでは健康診断の案内、スポーツクラブへの参加などが定番です。

Part 1 Photographs

DL 092, 093 CD2-50 CD2-51

Look at the picture and choose the statement that best describes what you see.

1. (A) (B) (C) (D)

2. (A) (B) (C) (D)

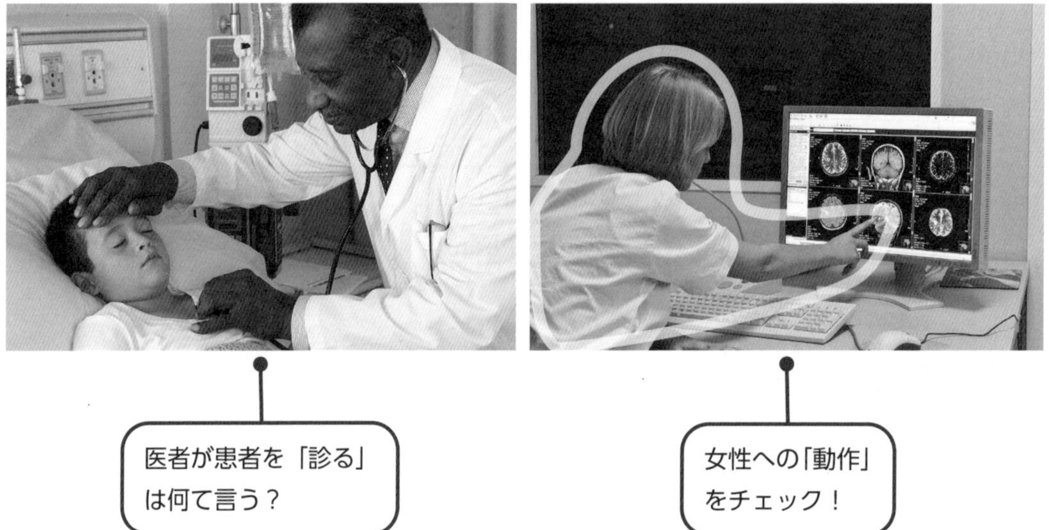

医者が患者を「診る」
は何て言う？
女性への「動作」
をチェック！

Part 2 Question-Response

DL 094 ~097 CD2-52 ~ CD2-55

Choose the best response to each question or statement.

3. (A) (B) (C)
4. (A) (B) (C)
5. (A) (B) (C)
6. (A) (B) (C)

Part 3 Short Conversations

DL 098, 099 CD2-56 ~ CD2-60

Listen to a short conversation, and choose the best answer to each question.

7. What is the purpose of the telephone call?

電話の「目的」！
セオリー通り、最初に注意！

   (A) To confirm a trip
   (B) To make an appointment
   (C) To join a course
   (D) To open an account

8. What does the woman request additionally?

女性の「追加」リクエストとは？

   (A) A free drink
   (B) To go alone
   (C) An extra test
   (D) A monthly report

9. When will the woman most likely visit the clinic?

When 設問はくせ者が多い！
ひっかけに注意しよう

   (A) Tomorrow afternoon
   (B) This week
   (C) Next Tuesday
   (D) Wednesday morning

Part 4 Short Talks

DL 100, 101

CD2-61 ~

CD2-64

Listen to a short talk, and choose the best answer to each question.

10. Where does the speaker probably work?

シチュエーションを推測しよう！

   (A) In a dental clinic
   (B) In a drug store
   (C) In a medical laboratory
   (D) At a cleaning service

11. What happened this morning?

何がトラブルかをつかむ

   (A) A tooth was extracted.
   (B) The office opened late.
   (C) A patient didn't show up for a check-up.
   (D) Someone visited a hospital.

12. What is the earliest that the listener can come again?

一番早く来れる日は？
「時間」表現に注意

   (A) This evening after 7 p.m.
   (B) Sometime this week
   (C) After the weekend
   (D) After next week

Unit 11

Finance & Banking

銀行はマイナー・トピック。通常のサービス表現がわかれば対応できます。財務関係は、リーディングは難所ですが、リスニングはそれほど難しくありません。

Part 1 Photographs

DL 102, 103　CD2-65　CD2-66

Look at the picture and choose the statement that best describes what you see.

1. (A)　(B)　(C)　(D)

「記入する」は何て言う？

2. (A)　(B)　(C)　(D)

「動作」に注目！

Part 2 Question-Response

DL 104～107　CD2-67 ～ CD2-70

Choose the best response to each question or statement.

3. (A)　(B)　(C)
4. (A)　(B)　(C)
5. (A)　(B)　(C)
6. (A)　(B)　(C)

「疑問詞」の正解率を上げよう！

Part 3 Short Conversations

DL 108, 109 CD2-71 ~ CD2-75

Listen to a short conversation, and choose the best answer to each question.

7. Where is the conversation taking place?

会話の「場所」→ 冒頭！

(A) In an IT department
(B) In a hotel lobby
(C) In a financial institute
(D) In an insurance firm

「トラブル」をキャッチしよう！

8. What is the man's problem?

(A) He can't get money.
(B) The worker hasn't been paid.
(C) The ATM isn't open.
(D) His card was stolen.

go next → 会話の最後に集中！

9. Where will the man most likely go next?

(A) The department store
(B) The cash dispenser
(C) The teller counter
(D) The vending machine

Part 4 Short Talks

DL 110, 111 

Listen to a short talk, and choose the best answer to each question.

10. Who is this advertisement aimed at?

広告のターゲットは誰？
冒頭から推測しよう！

(A) First-time customers
(B) Users for over 5 years
(C) Bank employees
(D) Overseas travelers

11. What service is being offered?

どんな「サービス」？
offer のあとにヒント！

(A) Competitive exchange rates
(B) Free financial advice
(C) High interest time deposit
(D) Special spending discounts

12. How should listeners apply for the offer?

〈How → By〉のパターン！
ウェブでの申込がよく出る

(A) By checking the newspaper for details
(B) By going online to register
(C) By sending an application form
(D) By waiting at least one year

Unit 12

Housing

住まい関連のトピックは意外とよく出ます。不動産屋とのやりとりでは、空き部屋情報や家賃、新築物件の見学案内など、大人な会話も頻出です。

Part 1 Photographs

DL 112, 113 CD2-80 CD2-81

Look at the picture and choose the statement that best describes what you see.

1. (A) (B) (C) (D)

2. (A) (B) (C) (D)

「位置・状態」を把握しよう！

「見下ろす」はよく出る！

Part 2 Question-Response

DL 114～117 CD2-82 ～ CD2-85

Choose the best response to each question or statement.

3. (A) (B) (C)
4. (A) (B) (C)
5. (A) (B) (C)
6. (A) (B) (C)

応答の「省略」に慣れよう！

Part 3 Short Conversations

DL 118, 119 CD2-86 ~ CD2-90

Listen to a short conversation, and choose the best answer to each question.

7. Who most likely is the woman?

女性の「職業」を冒頭から推測！

(A) A hotel receptionist
(B) A construction builder
(C) A real estate agent
(D) A housekeeper

8. What does the man ask for?

男性の「要望」を聞こう！

(A) A room with a great view
(B) 3 separate bedrooms
(C) A location closer to the workplace
(D) A spacious room

9. What will probably happen after this?

「次の展開」は会話の最後にヒント！

(A) The apartment will be renovated.
(B) The man will visit the property.
(C) The room will be shared.
(D) The price will be reduced.

Part 4 Short Talks

DL 120, 121 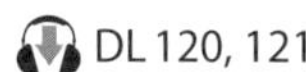 

Listen to a short talk, and choose the best answer to each question.

10. Who most likely is the listener?

メッセージの「聞き手」を推測しよう！

(A) A real-estate agent
(B) An office worker
(C) A parking attendant
(D) A security guard

11. According to the speaker, what has the listener requested?

聞き手の「要望」は？
部屋のタイプを聞き逃すな！

(A) A convenient residence
(B) A private terraced house
(C) A self-catering hotel room
(D) A country bungalow

12. When will the listener be in the area next?

next を見たら、
本文の最後に集中！

(A) The listener is already there
(B) When the branch opens
(C) Sometime next week
(D) In about 5 minutes

Unit 13

Media

ニュース関連は、交通情報を筆頭に、ビジネスニュースや新製品の紹介などが出題されます。ニュースは語彙が難しいので、リスニング最大の難所です。

Part 1 Photographs

DL 122, 123　CD3-02　CD3-03

Look at the picture and choose the statement that best describes what you see.

1. (A)　(B)　(C)　(D)

2. (A)　(B)　(C)　(D)

交通の定型表現が出る！

交通の「状態」を見よう！

Part 2 Question-Response

DL 124～127　CD3-04 ～ CD3-07

Choose the best response to each question or statement.

3. (A)　(B)　(C)
4. (A)　(B)　(C)
5. (A)　(B)　(C)
6. (A)　(B)　(C)

質問文が「平叙文（ふつうの文）」のときは難問が多い！

Part 3 Short Conversations

DL 128, 129 CD3-08 ~ CD3-15

Listen to a short conversation, and choose the best answer to each question.

7. Where does the conversation most likely take place?

   冒頭からシチュエーションをイメージ！

   (A) In a classroom
   (B) On a radio program
   (C) At a movie theater
   (D) At a restaurant

8. What does the woman imply when she says, "everyone in the film world is talking about it"?

   文脈理解が基本！

   (A) She is emphasizing the popularity of the film.
   (B) She is complaining about some of the scenes.
   (C) She is admitting she doesn't know much about the film.
   (D) She is describing how the movie was shot.

9. What do the women say about Jamie Chen?

   2人の女性
   →2人目は「同意」がセオリー！

   (A) He's popular because of his previous work.
   (B) He seems a bit young to play the title character.
   (C) He does a very good job in this role.
   (D) His performance is much like other roles he's played.

Part 4 Short Talks

DL 130, 131 CD3-16 ~ CD3-19

Listen to a short talk, and choose the best answer to each question.

10. What is the main topic of the news report?

ニュースの「主題」は何？

(A) The result of the campaign

(B) The birth of a new cub

(C) The renaming of the zoo

(D) The dates of the event

11. According to the report, what happened eight years ago?

名詞キーワード＝耳印！

(A) The zoo was founded.

(B) The panda got older.

(C) A panda cub was born.

(D) Zoo officials named the cub.

12. Why should visitors to the zoo come early?

Why 設問に注意！
「理由」のキャッチ
はかなり「難」！

(A) The weather is inclement.

(B) Many guests are expected.

(C) The number of tickets is limited.

(D) The zoo closes early.

Unit 14

Business

ビジネスは TOEIC の代名詞。会議トークやスピーチ、合併協議や商品発注など話題は多岐に及びます。仕事のシチュエーション把握がスコアアップの近道です。

Part 1 Photographs

Look at the picture and choose the statement that best describes what you see.

1. (A) (B) (C) (D)

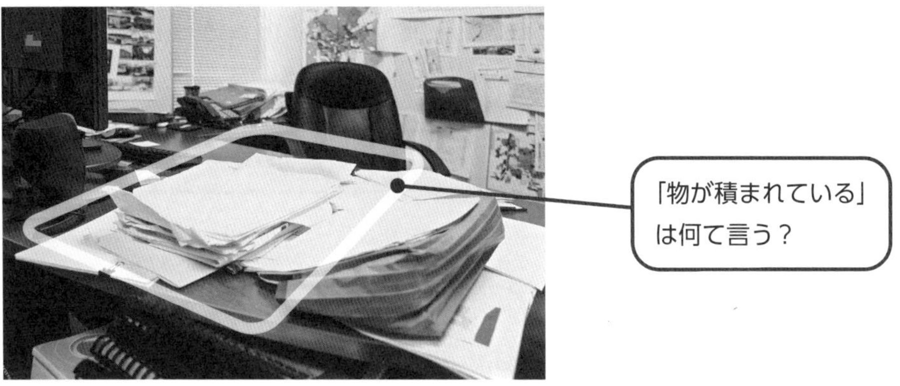

「物が積まれている」は何て言う？

2. (A) (B) (C) (D)

人物の「動作」をチェック！

Part 2 Question-Response

DL 134～137 CD3-22 ～ CD3-25

Choose the best response to each question or statement.

3. (A) (B) (C)

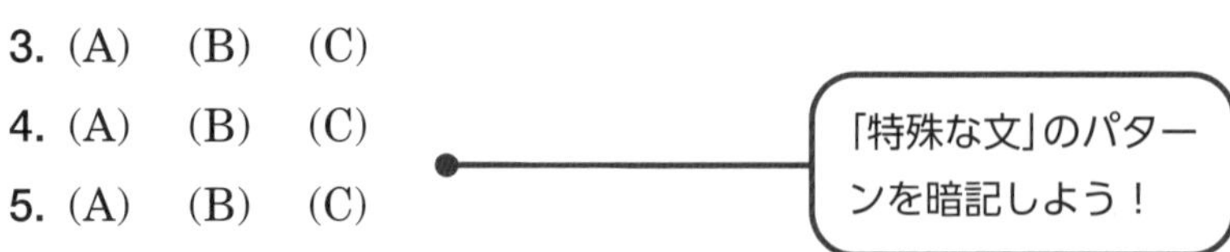
「特殊な文」のパターンを暗記しよう！

4. (A) (B) (C)
5. (A) (B) (C)
6. (A) (B) (C)

Part 3 Short Conversations

DL 138, 139
CD3-26 ～ CD3-30

Listen to a short conversation, and choose the best answer to each question.

7. Where is this conversation taking place?

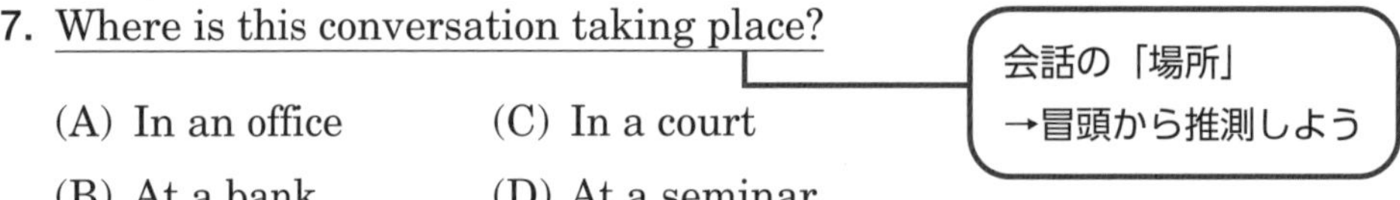
会話の「場所」
→冒頭から推測しよう

(A) In an office (C) In a court
(B) At a bank (D) At a seminar

8. What is the problem?

トラブル問題は、
「マイナス」のコメントを聞こう！

(A) The brochures have not arrived.
(B) The proposal is turned down.
(C) The details are not finalized yet.
(D) The software hasn't updated properly.

9. What does the woman want the man to do?

女性の「要望」は何？

(A) Get legal advice
(B) Expand business with the client
(C) Announce some news
(D) Get a document signed

Part 4 Short Talks

DL 140, 141 CD3-31 ~ CD3-34

Listen to a short talk, and choose the best answer to each question.

10. What problem does the speaker mention?

トラブルをキャッチしよう！

(A) The client cancelled their project.

(B) They have to change a project plan.

(C) They need to postpone a product campaign.

(D) They found a problem with a product.

11. Look at the graphic. In which slot is the speaker going to put their meeting?

図表は、選択肢にない情報を見よ！

Meeting Room Reservation (Dec 01)

	Room 1 (up to 6 people)	Room 2 (up to 12 people)
9 am – 11 am	New client support	Planning
1 pm – 3 pm	Management	Sales promotion

(A) Planning

(B) Management

(C) Sales promotion

(D) New client support

12. What will the listener probably do next?

聞き手の次の行動は？
→最後を聞こう！

(A) Check the schedule again

(B) Email the team

(C) Cancel the meeting

(D) Call the client

Unit 15

Reception Desk

受付でのやりとりは、ビジネスの定番です。何について話しているのかがわかれば簡単。基本表現を押さえるだけで、リスニング力は各段にアップします。

Part 1 Photographs

DL 142, 143　CD3-35　CD3-36

Look at the picture and choose the statement that best describes what you see.

1. (A)　(B)　(C)　(D)

2. (A)　(B)　(C)　(D)

2人の「位置」をチェック！

「向き合う」は定番表現！

Part 2 Question-Response

DL 144～147 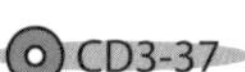 CD3-37 ～  CD3-40

Choose the best response to each question or statement.

3. (A)　(B)　(C)
4. (A)　(B)　(C)
5. (A)　(B)　(C)
6. (A)　(B)　(C)

Would you / Could you の「依頼文」は定番！

Part 3 Short Conversations

DL 148, 149 CD3-41 ~ CD3-45

Listen to a short conversation, and choose the best answer to each question.

7. Where does this conversation most likely take place?

会話の「場所」→ シチュエーションを把握しよう！

(A) On the telephone
(B) At a banquet hall
(C) At a reception counter
(D) At an insurance agency

8. Who most likely is Mr. Hammond?

Who 設問→「職業」を見抜け！

(A) The main secretary
(B) A receptionist
(C) A city official
(D) A company head

9. What will the woman do next?

do next → 本文 I'll ~ のパターン！

(A) Telephone her family
(B) Contact the vice-president
(C) Speak to a client
(D) Make a delivery

Part 4 Short Talks

DL150, 151 CD3-46 ~  CD3-49

Listen to a short talk, and choose the best answer to each question.

10. When will the business open again?

「日時」や「曜日」は言い換えに注意！

(A) 7 a.m. the next day
(B) 8:30 a.m. the next day
(C) 5 p.m. in the evening
(D) The day after tomorrow

11. What can visitors to the location enjoy tomorrow?

「プラス」の内容をキャッチしよう！

(A) A drink at a café
(B) A drive around the town
(C) A meal on the course
(D) A party at a club

12. How can listeners book the services offered?

予約の「方法」は？

(A) By buying lunch from the restaurant
(B) By turning up early in the morning
(C) By registering online at any time
(D) By calling again after 6 p.m.

Unit 16

Office Work

オフィスでは、様々なトピックに対応しなければなりません。会議、研修、人事、販売戦略、キャンペーンなど、トピックを意識することが大事です。

Part 1 Photographs

Look at the picture and choose the statement that best describes what you see.

1. (A) (B) (C) (D)

2. (A) (B) (C) (D)

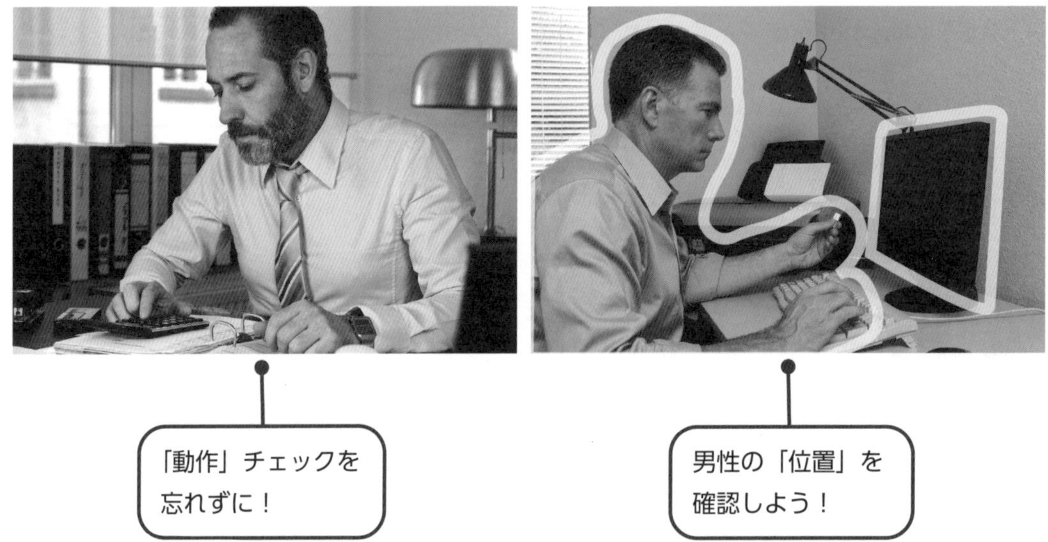

「動作」チェックを忘れずに！

男性の「位置」を確認しよう！

Part 2 Question-Response

Choose the best response to each question or statement.

3. (A) (B) (C)

4. (A) (B) (C)

5. (A) (B) (C)

6. (A) (B) (C)

「依頼文」への変則的な応答に注意！

Part 3 Short Conversations

DL 158, 159 CD3-56 ~ CD3-60

Listen to a short conversation, and choose the best answer to each question.

7. Why will the timecard system change?

   (A) To replace a broken machine
   (B) To improve the current system
   (C) To save more money
   (D) To manage employees better

システムを変える
「理由」とは？

8. What must be written by hand with the current system?

   (A) Order collections (C) Worker names
   (B) Mistakes (D) Adjustments

設問のポイントを見抜こう！
by hand がキーワード！

9. How does the man probably feel about the new system?

   (A) Excited (C) Nervous
   (B) Sad (D) Uncertain

「感情」問題は、プラス／マイナスで判断！

Part 4 Short Talks

DL160, 161 CD3-61 ~ CD3-64 

Listen to a short talk, and choose the best answer to each question.

10. Who most likely is the speaker?

    (A) A product designer
    (B) A company executive
    (C) A radio host
    (D) An advertising agent

「話し手」は誰？
意外な人物であることも！

「日付」「数字」は、耳印にしよう！

11. What happened on March 23?

    (A) A store was established. (C) An item went on sale.
    (B) A product was bought out. (D) A newspaper was published.

12. What are the sales results?

    (A) Less profit than expected
    (B) Much higher than anticipated
    (C) It's a big announcement
    (D) The same as last year

セールの「結果」は？
アナウンスの後半から推測！

Unit 17

Employment & Personnel

人事はビジネスパーソンの一大事。昇任、転勤（異動）、退職、採用面接、新人研修など、人事トピックは豊富です。就任・退職スピーチも常連ですね。

Part 1 Photographs

DL 162, 163 CD3-65 CD3-66

Look at the picture and choose the statement that best describes what you see.

1. (A) (B) (C) (D)

2. (A) (B) (C) (D)

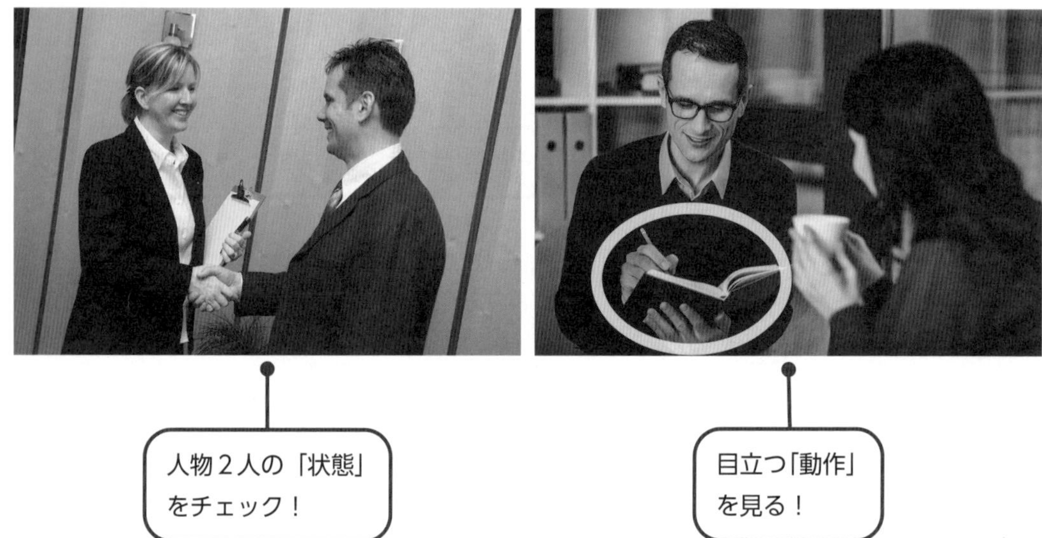

Part 2 Question-Response

DL 164～167 CD3-67 ～ CD3-70

Choose the best response to each question or statement.

3. (A) (B) (C)
4. (A) (B) (C)
5. (A) (B) (C)
6. (A) (B) (C)

間接疑問文の「疑問詞」をキャッチ！

Part 3 Short Conversations

DL 168, 169 CD3-71 ~ CD3-75

Listen to a short conversation, and choose the best answer to each question.

7. Why did the man contact the woman?

Why 設問→「理由」をキャッチ！

(A) To apply to a job position
(B) To inquire about finances
(C) To respond to an application
(D) To return a telephone call

8. When will the speakers most likely meet?

most likely →「推測」のサイン

(A) Tuesday morning (C) Wednesday morning
(B) Tuesday afternoon (D) Wednesday afternoon

9. According to the man, what should the woman bring to the meeting?

ミーティングに持ってくる「モノ」は何？

(A) A claim form (C) A questionnaire
(B) Nothing in particular (D) Job references

Part 4 Short Talks

Listen to a short talk, and choose the best answer to each question.

10. How many months has Nathan Monday set a sales record?

「数字」問題はトリッキー！

(A) Two months (C) Five months
(B) Four months (D) Six months

11. What does the speaker say Nathan Monday has done since he was hired?

人名＝名詞キーワード！

(A) Surpassed monthly sales targets
(B) Hired employees
(C) Gave an achievement award
(D) Represented his department

12. What will the participants do next?

定番の do next ！
スピーチの最後を聞こう

(A) Keep up the good work
(B) Report new sales figures
(C) Go to the stage
(D) Listen to a speech

Unit 18

Office Announcement

オフィスアナウンスは、社内連絡のようなものです。社内の工事案内、会議やパーティの案内、旅費規程の改定など、社員へのお知らせと思えば簡単ですね。

Part 1 Photographs

DL 172, 173　CD3-80　CD3-81

Look at the picture and choose the statement that best describes what you see.

1. (A)　(B)　(C)　(D)

「ガランとした部屋」は何て言う？

2. (A)　(B)　(C)　(D)

2人の「位置」関係をチェック！

Part 2 Question-Response

DL 174～177　CD3-82 ～ CD3-85

Choose the best response to each question or statement.

3. (A)　(B)　(C)
4. (A)　(B)　(C)
5. (A)　(B)　(C)
6. (A)　(B)　(C)

「平叙文」への様々な応答に対応しよう

Part 3 Short Conversations

DL 178, 179 CD3-86 ~ CD3-90

Listen to a short conversation, and choose the best answer to each question.

7. What will be happening in the office tomorrow?
   (A) The speakers will work overtime.
   (B) Electricians will come in.
   (C) The office will close at 9 p.m.
   (D) The manager will have a meeting.

明日の「出来事」→
未来表現にヒント！

8. What is the problem for the two speakers?
   (A) They haven't received the documents.
   (B) They will do some repair work.
   (C) They have to complete the work tonight.
   (D) The computer needs to be fixed.

トラブル問題では
「マイナス」をキャッチ！

9. What will the woman most likely do after this?
   (A) Call her spouse
   (B) Send an e-mail
   (C) Talk to the repair person
   (D) Go straight home

定番の do (next) ！
会話の最後にヒント

Part 4 Short Talks

DL180, 181 CD3-91 ~ 

Listen to a short talk, and choose the best answer to each question.

10. What does the speaker remind listeners about today?
   (A) A school will be opened.
   (B) Many customers are coming.
   (C) An arts festival will be held.
   (D) The center will close early.

remind = tell とすれば簡単！
設問のリーディングは大事

定番の Who 設問！→「職業」を聞こう

11. Who is Jackie Dee?
   (A) A famous musician
   (B) A family member
   (C) A regular customer
   (D) A well-known writer

12. What does the speaker suggest available staff do at 3 p.m.?
   (A) Gather for a meeting
   (B) Sign up for overtime
   (C) Do a stock-take
   (D) Help with crowd control

どんな staff ？
available の解釈が重要

Unit 19

Office Talk

オフィストークは、ビジネスからプライベートに至るまで、様々な内容が含まれます。同僚とのおしゃべりをイメージすればわかりやすいでしょう。

Part 1 Photographs

DL 182, 183　CD4-02　CD4-03

Look at the picture and choose the statement that best describes what you see.

1. (A)　(B)　(C)　(D)

2. (A)　(B)　(C)　(D)

3人でも「共通点」をチェック！
「向き合う」は出る！

Part 2 Question-Response

DL 184～187　CD4-04 ～ CD4-07

Choose the best response to each question or statement.

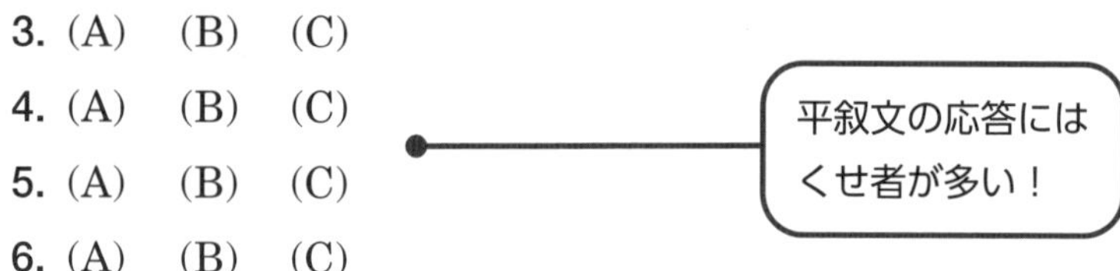
3. (A)　(B)　(C)
4. (A)　(B)　(C)
5. (A)　(B)　(C)
6. (A)　(B)　(C)
平叙文の応答にはくせ者が多い！

Part 3 Short Conversations

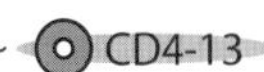

Listen to a short conversation, and choose the best answer to each question.

7. What do they say about moving to a new office building?

オフィス移転の感想は？
→プラス／マイナスでとらえる

(A) All the floors of the departments will have great views.
(B) Construction costs have put pressure on the company.
(C) Internal communication will be better and easier.
(D) Moving is too much extra work for the employees.

8. Look at the graphic. Which Zone is the man going to move to?

Zone 1	1st through 5th floors
Zone 2	6th through 19th floors
Zone 3	20th through 35th floors
Zone 4	36th through 40th floors

選択肢にない情報
＝「階数」がヒント！

(A) Zone 1
(B) Zone 2
(C) Zone 3
(D) Zone 4

9. What is the woman probably going to do next?

do next 問題
→会話の最後にヒント

(A) Visit the man's floor to get a document
(B) Find out which floor she will move to
(C) Check out the view from an upper floor
(D) Have a meeting of all employees in one place

Part 4 Short Talks

DL 190, 191　CD4-14 ~ CD4-17

Listen to a short talk, and choose the best answer to each question.

10. What is the main purpose of the announcement?

アナウンスの「目的」！
冒頭をチェック

(A) To advertise an apartment

(B) To inform changes in rules

(C) To redesign the staff room

(D) To explain new facilities

11. Why has the new room been offered for the staff?

「理由」をしっかり
キャッチしよう

(A) To arrange for lunch

(B) To shorten work hours

(C) To provide a space for smokers

(D) To increase work performance

12. Who will have to keep the area clean?

設問リーディングが重要！

(A) The managers

(B) A cleaning service

(C) Every staff member

(D) New employees

Unit 20

New Products

(新)製品については、店頭ディスプレイや工場写真が定番です。
オフィスでの売上トークや店頭の販売トークに加え、ラジオＣＭなどでも扱われます。

Part 1 Photographs

Look at the picture and choose the statement that best describes what you see.

1. (A)　(B)　(C)　(D)

2. (A)　(B)　(C)　(D)

「展示」では arrange や display を待ち伏せよう

Part 2 Question-Response

DL 194～197 CD4-20 ～ CD4-23

Choose the best response to each question or statement.

3. (A) (B) (C)
4. (A) (B) (C)
5. (A) (B) (C)
6. (A) (B) (C)

応答が「疑問文」のパターンをマスターしよう！

Part 3 Short Conversations

DL 198, 199 CD4-24 ～ CD4-28

Listen to a short conversation, and choose the best answer to each question.

7. Who are the two speakers?

話し手の「職業」をイメージして！

(A) Package designers
(B) Restaurant workers
(C) Department colleagues
(D) Food manufacturers

8. How will the product name be decided?

製品の名前の「決め方」は？

(A) By public vote
(B) Through TV advertising
(C) By matching it to other product names
(D) By asking the employees

9. What will the woman most likely do next?

定番の do next ！本文の最後を聞こう

(A) Enter a competition
(B) E-mail workers for their ideas
(C) Make the product package
(D) Test the taste of the food

Part 4 Short Talks

DL 200, 201  ~ 

Listen to a short talk, and choose the best answer to each question.

10. What is E-drive?

どんな会社かをつかむ

(A) A retail store selling smartphones

(B) A hard drive for storing data

(C) A new product for taking videos

(D) A company offering a new storage service

11. What does the speaker mean when he says, "we'd like to appeal to another market segment?"

ターゲット文の後を聞こう！

(A) They only want to sell to businesses.

(B) They want older people to use their service.

(C) They want their product to be available for research.

(D) They don't think students should pay for the service.

12. What does the speaker say is special about the new product?

special（=売り）をキャッチする

(A) It can be used outside the home.

(B) It comes with a long-term guarantee.

(C) It's cheap and easy to operate.

(D) It's reliable and flexible.

Unit 21

Sales

TOEIC はセールが大好き。いつもセールをしている印象があります。店頭のセール写真やトーク、販売戦略に関するオフィストークが頻出です。

Part 1 Photographs

Look at the picture and choose the statement that best describes what you see.

1. (A) (B) (C) (D)

2. (A) (B) (C) (D)

「見る」は
look だけではない

「展示」の
頻出表現は？

Part 2 Question-Response

DL 204～207  ～ 

Choose the best response to each question or statement.

3. (A) (B) (C)
4. (A) (B) (C)
5. (A) (B) (C)
6. (A) (B) (C)

「提案・勧誘」の定番表現を
マスターしよう！

Part 3 Short Conversations

DL 208, 209 

Listen to a short conversation, and choose the best answer to each question.

7. Where is the conversation probably taking place?

会話の「場所」は冒頭！

(A) At a department store
(B) At a restaurant
(C) At a post office
(D) At a newspaper stand

8. What is the problem with the coupon?

クーポンの「問題」は何？

(A) It is out of date.
(B) Spending needs to be over a certain amount.
(C) It can only be used at a certain branch.
(D) A member's card is needed.

9. What does the woman suggest the man do?

女性の「提案」をキャッチしよう
会話の最後に注意！

(A) Become a member
(B) Buy the goods today
(C) Visit another branch
(D) Subscribe to a paper

Part 4 Short Talks

DL210, 211 

~ 

Listen to a short talk, and choose the best answer to each question.

10. In what type of business is the speaker working?

どんなビジネス
=「業種」？

(A) A grocery store
(B) A health-oriented eatery
(C) A vegetable farming
(D) A gift center

11. What is one of the new items being offered?

新商品は何？
設問をシンプルに
理解して！

(A) A fruit juice
(B) A hot herbal tea
(C) A variety of snack bars
(D) An iced yogurt

12. How do customers receive a free gift?

free gift の受取方法は？

(A) By making a one-time purchase
(B) By giving a product review
(C) By using a coupon
(D) By showing proof of multiple visits

Unit 22

Seminar & Meeting

会議やセミナーは、ビジネスと相性抜群。会議写真はおなじみですね。ですが、会議室でのビジネストークは多岐に及ぶので注意が必要です。

Part 1 Photographs

DL 212, 213  CD4-48  CD4-49

Look at the picture and choose the statement that best describes what you see.

1. (A)　(B)　(C)　(D)

2. (A)　(B)　(C)　(D)

全員の「共通点」をチェック！

イスの「並び」に注目！

Part 2 Question-Response

DL 214～217 CD4-50 ～  CD4-53

Choose the best response to each question or statement.

3. (A)　(B)　(C)
4. (A)　(B)　(C)
5. (A)　(B)　(C)
6. (A)　(B)　(C)

Q（否定疑問文）→ A（難応答）のパターン！

Part 3 Short Conversations

Listen to a short conversation, and choose the best answer to each question.

7. What is going to start on Thursdays?

講座/クラスの種類を見抜こう

(A) Trips abroad
(B) An exchange program
(C) Language classes
(D) Art lessons

8. Why is the woman reluctant to attend the course?

気の進まない理由は何？

(A) She's never studied French.
(B) She doesn't want to go on her own.
(C) She's forgotten what she learned.
(D) She doesn't have much time.

9. What does the man suggest the woman do?

男性の「提案」をキャッチ！

(A) Visit Paris
(B) Register full-time
(C) Wait three months
(D) Attend the class

Part 4 Short Talks

Listen to a short talk, and choose the best answer to each question.

10. Who is the talk addressed to?

トークの「対象」は？
設問の意味をとらえて！

(A) New company employees
(B) Investors in the organization
(C) Leaders in the community
(D) Columbus committee

11. What will HIO direct their attention to this year?

HIO は何に注目している？

(A) Enriching the surrounding community
(B) Expanding after-school programs
(C) Growing the company in new markets
(D) Holding workshops about community service

12. What most likely will happen next?

「次の展開」は、
トークの最後を聞こう！

(A) The speakers will introduce themselves.
(B) The attendees will begin to leave.
(C) A question and answer session will start.
(D) The workshops will start.

Unit 23

Logistics

運輸・流通は、倉庫写真や在庫トークに顕著です。
交通トピックとも関連するので、頻出表現はまとめて覚えておくと便利です。

Part 1 Photographs

Look at the picture and choose the statement that best describes what you see.

1. (A) (B) (C) (D)

2. (A) (B) (C) (D)

「箱が積まれている」は何て言う？
「船」の状態に注目！

Part 2 Question-Response

Choose the best response to each question or statement.

3. (A) (B) (C)
4. (A) (B) (C)
5. (A) (B) (C)
6. (A) (B) (C)

「How」は頻出！
ヴァリエーションをチェック！

Part 3 Short Conversations

DL 228, 229 CD4-69 ～ CD4-73

Listen to a short conversation, and choose the best answer to each question.

7. What is the purpose of the call?

電話の「目的」！
→セオリー通り、冒頭にヒント！

(A) To sell office materials
(B) To store important documents
(C) To inquire about a price quote
(D) To receive company details

8. What will happen to the filing cabinets?

名詞キーワードをチェック！

(A) They will be removed while remodeling.
(B) Someone will keep them in the store.
(C) A repair person will fix them.
(D) They will stay where they are.

9. What does the man say he will do next?

定番の do next！→取りこぼし厳禁！

(A) Revise the prices
(B) Increase the cost
(C) Move cabinets
(D) Find an old estimate

Part 4 Short Talks

DL230, 231 

Listen to a short talk, and choose the best answer to each question.

10. What type of business is the speaker working in?

仕事のジャンルは、
選択肢「タテ読み」が効果的

(A) An insurance agency
(B) An academic institute
(C) A staff training company
(D) A professional moving company

11. What is the reason for the insurance?

キーワードを耳印に、ヒントを聞こう

(A) To cover the cost of travel
(B) To pay for lost or damaged property
(C) To help with employment costs
(D) To assist with medical expenses

12. Who can get discounts?

割引の「対象者」は誰？

(A) Workers to be transferred overseas
(B) New graduates
(C) Students entering college
(D) Company employees

Unit 24

Construction & Production

TOEIC は工事や作業が大好き。工事現場や野外作業の写真に加え、社内工事や公共施設の改修トークなど、ガテン系トピックが頻出です。

Part 1 Photographs

DL 232, 233 CD4-78 CD4-79

Look at the picture and choose the statement that best describes what you see.

1. (A) (B) (C) (D)

「カートを押す」は何て言う？

2. (A) (B) (C) (D)

「重機」は定番表現！

Part 2 Question-Response

DL 234～237 CD4-80 ～ CD4-83

Choose the best response to each question or statement.

3. (A) (B) (C)
4. (A) (B) (C)
5. (A) (B) (C)
6. (A) (B) (C)

「疑問詞」の最終チェックをしよう！

Part 3 Short Conversations

DL 238, 239 CD4-84 ~ CD4-88

Listen to a short conversation, and choose the best answer to each question.

7. What will happen on the 19th? ——「日付」を耳印に、その周辺を聞こう
   (A) There will be no gas.
   (B) The street will be blocked.
   (C) The woman won't use her car.
   (D) A neighborhood party will take place.

8. What did the man give the woman? —— 男性が手渡したモノは？
   (A) A complimentary pass
   (B) A parking fine
   (C) A resident card
   (D) A recommendation letter

9. What does the man suggest the woman do? —— 難設問の suggest ！男性の「提案」を聞こう！
   (A) Arrange for paid parking
   (B) Leave home early
   (C) Move the vehicle a day before
   (D) Take alternative transport

Part 4 Short Talks

DL240, 241 CD4-89 ~ CD4-92

Listen to a short talk, and choose the best answer to each question.

10. What is the main purpose of the talk? —— トークの「目的」！冒頭以外にヒントがあるケースも！
    (A) To notify that building work will affect business
    (B) To inform of complaints from customers
    (C) To request closure of the building
    (D) To remind staff of a change in the transport system

11. What is the problem with Maypole Street? —— キーワードを耳印に、トラブルをキャッチ！
    (A) There is no parking available.
    (B) Customers have to use the East gate.
    (C) The door of the entrance can't be opened.
    (D) There will be construction vehicles parked on it.

12. What does the speaker want employees to do? —— want 問題では話し手の「要望」をつかむ
    (A) Meet clients at other locations
    (B) Help visitors choose a service
    (C) Tell customers about building access
    (D) Contact the construction company

本書にはCD（別売）があります

SHOOT UP TO THE TOEIC® TEST LISTENING

解法のコツを極める TOEIC®テストリスニング演習

2024年1月20日　初版第1刷発行
2024年2月20日　初版第2刷発行

著　者　　塚田　幸光

発行者　　福岡　正人

発行所　株式会社　**金星堂**

（〒101-0051）東京都千代田区神田神保町 3-21
Tel　(03) 3263-3828（営業部）
　　　(03) 3263-3997（編集部）
Fax　(03) 3263-0716
https://www.kinsei-do.co.jp

編集担当　稲葉真美香　　Printed in Japan
印刷所・製本所／倉敷印刷株式会社

ISBN978-4-7647-4208-6　C1082

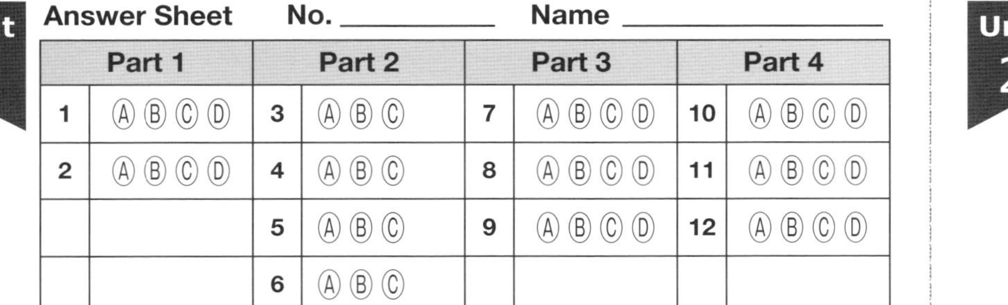

Unit 1

Answer Sheet No. ________ Name ____________

Part 1		Part 2		Part 3		Part 4	
1	Ⓐ Ⓑ Ⓒ Ⓓ	3	Ⓐ Ⓑ Ⓒ	7	Ⓐ Ⓑ Ⓒ Ⓓ	10	Ⓐ Ⓑ Ⓒ Ⓓ
2	Ⓐ Ⓑ Ⓒ Ⓓ	4	Ⓐ Ⓑ Ⓒ	8	Ⓐ Ⓑ Ⓒ Ⓓ	11	Ⓐ Ⓑ Ⓒ Ⓓ
		5	Ⓐ Ⓑ Ⓒ	9	Ⓐ Ⓑ Ⓒ Ⓓ	12	Ⓐ Ⓑ Ⓒ Ⓓ
		6	Ⓐ Ⓑ Ⓒ				

SHOOT UP TO THE TOEIC® TEST LISTENING

Unit 2

Answer Sheet No. ________ Name ____________

Part 1		Part 2		Part 3		Part 4	
1	Ⓐ Ⓑ Ⓒ Ⓓ	3	Ⓐ Ⓑ Ⓒ	7	Ⓐ Ⓑ Ⓒ Ⓓ	10	Ⓐ Ⓑ Ⓒ Ⓓ
2	Ⓐ Ⓑ Ⓒ Ⓓ	4	Ⓐ Ⓑ Ⓒ	8	Ⓐ Ⓑ Ⓒ Ⓓ	11	Ⓐ Ⓑ Ⓒ Ⓓ
		5	Ⓐ Ⓑ Ⓒ	9	Ⓐ Ⓑ Ⓒ Ⓓ	12	Ⓐ Ⓑ Ⓒ Ⓓ
		6	Ⓐ Ⓑ Ⓒ				

SHOOT UP TO THE TOEIC® TEST LISTENING

Unit 3

Answer Sheet No. ________ Name ____________

Part 1		Part 2		Part 3		Part 4	
1	Ⓐ Ⓑ Ⓒ Ⓓ	3	Ⓐ Ⓑ Ⓒ	7	Ⓐ Ⓑ Ⓒ Ⓓ	10	Ⓐ Ⓑ Ⓒ Ⓓ
2	Ⓐ Ⓑ Ⓒ Ⓓ	4	Ⓐ Ⓑ Ⓒ	8	Ⓐ Ⓑ Ⓒ Ⓓ	11	Ⓐ Ⓑ Ⓒ Ⓓ
		5	Ⓐ Ⓑ Ⓒ	9	Ⓐ Ⓑ Ⓒ Ⓓ	12	Ⓐ Ⓑ Ⓒ Ⓓ
		6	Ⓐ Ⓑ Ⓒ				

SHOOT UP TO THE TOEIC® TEST LISTENING

Unit 4

Answer Sheet No. ________ Name ____________

Part 1		Part 2		Part 3		Part 4	
1	Ⓐ Ⓑ Ⓒ Ⓓ	3	Ⓐ Ⓑ Ⓒ	7	Ⓐ Ⓑ Ⓒ Ⓓ	10	Ⓐ Ⓑ Ⓒ Ⓓ
2	Ⓐ Ⓑ Ⓒ Ⓓ	4	Ⓐ Ⓑ Ⓒ	8	Ⓐ Ⓑ Ⓒ Ⓓ	11	Ⓐ Ⓑ Ⓒ Ⓓ
		5	Ⓐ Ⓑ Ⓒ	9	Ⓐ Ⓑ Ⓒ Ⓓ	12	Ⓐ Ⓑ Ⓒ Ⓓ
		6	Ⓐ Ⓑ Ⓒ				

SHOOT UP TO THE TOEIC® TEST LISTENING

Unit 5

Answer Sheet No. ________ Name ____________

Part 1		Part 2		Part 3		Part 4	
1	Ⓐ Ⓑ Ⓒ Ⓓ	3	Ⓐ Ⓑ Ⓒ	7	Ⓐ Ⓑ Ⓒ Ⓓ	10	Ⓐ Ⓑ Ⓒ Ⓓ
2	Ⓐ Ⓑ Ⓒ Ⓓ	4	Ⓐ Ⓑ Ⓒ	8	Ⓐ Ⓑ Ⓒ Ⓓ	11	Ⓐ Ⓑ Ⓒ Ⓓ
		5	Ⓐ Ⓑ Ⓒ	9	Ⓐ Ⓑ Ⓒ Ⓓ	12	Ⓐ Ⓑ Ⓒ Ⓓ
		6	Ⓐ Ⓑ Ⓒ				

SHOOT UP TO THE TOEIC® TEST LISTENING

Unit 6

Answer Sheet No. ________ Name ____________

Part 1		Part 2		Part 3		Part 4	
1	Ⓐ Ⓑ Ⓒ Ⓓ	3	Ⓐ Ⓑ Ⓒ	7	Ⓐ Ⓑ Ⓒ Ⓓ	10	Ⓐ Ⓑ Ⓒ Ⓓ
2	Ⓐ Ⓑ Ⓒ Ⓓ	4	Ⓐ Ⓑ Ⓒ	8	Ⓐ Ⓑ Ⓒ Ⓓ	11	Ⓐ Ⓑ Ⓒ Ⓓ
		5	Ⓐ Ⓑ Ⓒ	9	Ⓐ Ⓑ Ⓒ Ⓓ	12	Ⓐ Ⓑ Ⓒ Ⓓ
		6	Ⓐ Ⓑ Ⓒ				

SHOOT UP TO THE TOEIC® TEST LISTENING

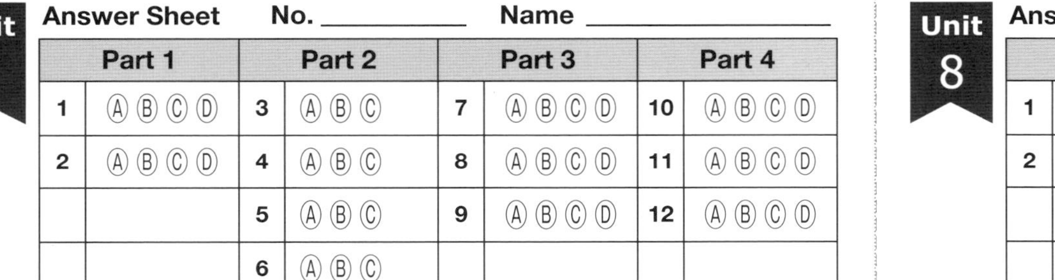

Unit 7

Answer Sheet No. ______ Name ______

Part 1		Part 2		Part 3		Part 4	
1	Ⓐ Ⓑ Ⓒ Ⓓ	3	Ⓐ Ⓑ Ⓒ	7	Ⓐ Ⓑ Ⓒ Ⓓ	10	Ⓐ Ⓑ Ⓒ Ⓓ
2	Ⓐ Ⓑ Ⓒ Ⓓ	4	Ⓐ Ⓑ Ⓒ	8	Ⓐ Ⓑ Ⓒ Ⓓ	11	Ⓐ Ⓑ Ⓒ Ⓓ
		5	Ⓐ Ⓑ Ⓒ	9	Ⓐ Ⓑ Ⓒ Ⓓ	12	Ⓐ Ⓑ Ⓒ Ⓓ
		6	Ⓐ Ⓑ Ⓒ				

SHOOT UP TO THE TOEIC® TEST LISTENING

Unit 8

Answer Sheet No. ______ Name ______

Part 1		Part 2		Part 3		Part 4	
1	Ⓐ Ⓑ Ⓒ Ⓓ	3	Ⓐ Ⓑ Ⓒ	7	Ⓐ Ⓑ Ⓒ Ⓓ	10	Ⓐ Ⓑ Ⓒ Ⓓ
2	Ⓐ Ⓑ Ⓒ Ⓓ	4	Ⓐ Ⓑ Ⓒ	8	Ⓐ Ⓑ Ⓒ Ⓓ	11	Ⓐ Ⓑ Ⓒ Ⓓ
		5	Ⓐ Ⓑ Ⓒ	9	Ⓐ Ⓑ Ⓒ Ⓓ	12	Ⓐ Ⓑ Ⓒ Ⓓ
		6	Ⓐ Ⓑ Ⓒ				

SHOOT UP TO THE TOEIC® TEST LISTENING

Unit 9

Answer Sheet No. ______ Name ______

Part 1		Part 2		Part 3		Part 4	
1	Ⓐ Ⓑ Ⓒ Ⓓ	3	Ⓐ Ⓑ Ⓒ	7	Ⓐ Ⓑ Ⓒ Ⓓ	10	Ⓐ Ⓑ Ⓒ Ⓓ
2	Ⓐ Ⓑ Ⓒ Ⓓ	4	Ⓐ Ⓑ Ⓒ	8	Ⓐ Ⓑ Ⓒ Ⓓ	11	Ⓐ Ⓑ Ⓒ Ⓓ
		5	Ⓐ Ⓑ Ⓒ	9	Ⓐ Ⓑ Ⓒ Ⓓ	12	Ⓐ Ⓑ Ⓒ Ⓓ
		6	Ⓐ Ⓑ Ⓒ				

SHOOT UP TO THE TOEIC® TEST LISTENING

Unit 10

Answer Sheet No. ______ Name ______

Part 1		Part 2		Part 3		Part 4	
1	Ⓐ Ⓑ Ⓒ Ⓓ	3	Ⓐ Ⓑ Ⓒ	7	Ⓐ Ⓑ Ⓒ Ⓓ	10	Ⓐ Ⓑ Ⓒ Ⓓ
2	Ⓐ Ⓑ Ⓒ Ⓓ	4	Ⓐ Ⓑ Ⓒ	8	Ⓐ Ⓑ Ⓒ Ⓓ	11	Ⓐ Ⓑ Ⓒ Ⓓ
		5	Ⓐ Ⓑ Ⓒ	9	Ⓐ Ⓑ Ⓒ Ⓓ	12	Ⓐ Ⓑ Ⓒ Ⓓ
		6	Ⓐ Ⓑ Ⓒ				

SHOOT UP TO THE TOEIC® TEST LISTENING

Unit 11

Answer Sheet No. ______ Name ______

Part 1		Part 2		Part 3		Part 4	
1	Ⓐ Ⓑ Ⓒ Ⓓ	3	Ⓐ Ⓑ Ⓒ	7	Ⓐ Ⓑ Ⓒ Ⓓ	10	Ⓐ Ⓑ Ⓒ Ⓓ
2	Ⓐ Ⓑ Ⓒ Ⓓ	4	Ⓐ Ⓑ Ⓒ	8	Ⓐ Ⓑ Ⓒ Ⓓ	11	Ⓐ Ⓑ Ⓒ Ⓓ
		5	Ⓐ Ⓑ Ⓒ	9	Ⓐ Ⓑ Ⓒ Ⓓ	12	Ⓐ Ⓑ Ⓒ Ⓓ
		6	Ⓐ Ⓑ Ⓒ				

SHOOT UP TO THE TOEIC® TEST LISTENING

Unit 12

Answer Sheet No. ______ Name ______

Part 1		Part 2		Part 3		Part 4	
1	Ⓐ Ⓑ Ⓒ Ⓓ	3	Ⓐ Ⓑ Ⓒ	7	Ⓐ Ⓑ Ⓒ Ⓓ	10	Ⓐ Ⓑ Ⓒ Ⓓ
2	Ⓐ Ⓑ Ⓒ Ⓓ	4	Ⓐ Ⓑ Ⓒ	8	Ⓐ Ⓑ Ⓒ Ⓓ	11	Ⓐ Ⓑ Ⓒ Ⓓ
		5	Ⓐ Ⓑ Ⓒ	9	Ⓐ Ⓑ Ⓒ Ⓓ	12	Ⓐ Ⓑ Ⓒ Ⓓ
		6	Ⓐ Ⓑ Ⓒ				

SHOOT UP TO THE TOEIC® TEST LISTENING

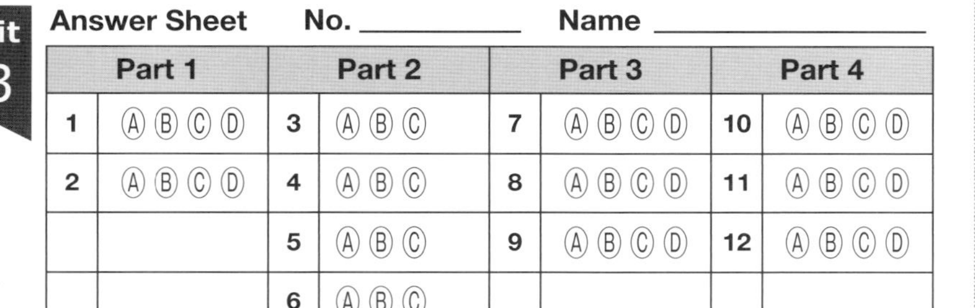

Unit 13 Answer Sheet No. ______ Name ______

Part 1		Part 2		Part 3		Part 4	
1	Ⓐ Ⓑ Ⓒ Ⓓ	3	Ⓐ Ⓑ Ⓒ	7	Ⓐ Ⓑ Ⓒ Ⓓ	10	Ⓐ Ⓑ Ⓒ Ⓓ
2	Ⓐ Ⓑ Ⓒ Ⓓ	4	Ⓐ Ⓑ Ⓒ	8	Ⓐ Ⓑ Ⓒ Ⓓ	11	Ⓐ Ⓑ Ⓒ Ⓓ
		5	Ⓐ Ⓑ Ⓒ	9	Ⓐ Ⓑ Ⓒ Ⓓ	12	Ⓐ Ⓑ Ⓒ Ⓓ
		6	Ⓐ Ⓑ Ⓒ				

SHOOT UP TO THE TOEIC® TEST LISTENING

Unit 14 Answer Sheet No. ______ Name ______

Part 1		Part 2		Part 3		Part 4	
1	Ⓐ Ⓑ Ⓒ Ⓓ	3	Ⓐ Ⓑ Ⓒ	7	Ⓐ Ⓑ Ⓒ Ⓓ	10	Ⓐ Ⓑ Ⓒ Ⓓ
2	Ⓐ Ⓑ Ⓒ Ⓓ	4	Ⓐ Ⓑ Ⓒ	8	Ⓐ Ⓑ Ⓒ Ⓓ	11	Ⓐ Ⓑ Ⓒ Ⓓ
		5	Ⓐ Ⓑ Ⓒ	9	Ⓐ Ⓑ Ⓒ Ⓓ	12	Ⓐ Ⓑ Ⓒ Ⓓ
		6	Ⓐ Ⓑ Ⓒ				

SHOOT UP TO THE TOEIC® TEST LISTENING

Unit 15 Answer Sheet No. ______ Name ______

Part 1		Part 2		Part 3		Part 4	
1	Ⓐ Ⓑ Ⓒ Ⓓ	3	Ⓐ Ⓑ Ⓒ	7	Ⓐ Ⓑ Ⓒ Ⓓ	10	Ⓐ Ⓑ Ⓒ Ⓓ
2	Ⓐ Ⓑ Ⓒ Ⓓ	4	Ⓐ Ⓑ Ⓒ	8	Ⓐ Ⓑ Ⓒ Ⓓ	11	Ⓐ Ⓑ Ⓒ Ⓓ
		5	Ⓐ Ⓑ Ⓒ	9	Ⓐ Ⓑ Ⓒ Ⓓ	12	Ⓐ Ⓑ Ⓒ Ⓓ
		6	Ⓐ Ⓑ Ⓒ				

SHOOT UP TO THE TOEIC® TEST LISTENING

Unit 16 Answer Sheet No. ______ Name ______

Part 1		Part 2		Part 3		Part 4	
1	Ⓐ Ⓑ Ⓒ Ⓓ	3	Ⓐ Ⓑ Ⓒ	7	Ⓐ Ⓑ Ⓒ Ⓓ	10	Ⓐ Ⓑ Ⓒ Ⓓ
2	Ⓐ Ⓑ Ⓒ Ⓓ	4	Ⓐ Ⓑ Ⓒ	8	Ⓐ Ⓑ Ⓒ Ⓓ	11	Ⓐ Ⓑ Ⓒ Ⓓ
		5	Ⓐ Ⓑ Ⓒ	9	Ⓐ Ⓑ Ⓒ Ⓓ	12	Ⓐ Ⓑ Ⓒ Ⓓ
		6	Ⓐ Ⓑ Ⓒ				

SHOOT UP TO THE TOEIC® TEST LISTENING

Unit 17 Answer Sheet No. ______ Name ______

Part 1		Part 2		Part 3		Part 4	
1	Ⓐ Ⓑ Ⓒ Ⓓ	3	Ⓐ Ⓑ Ⓒ	7	Ⓐ Ⓑ Ⓒ Ⓓ	10	Ⓐ Ⓑ Ⓒ Ⓓ
2	Ⓐ Ⓑ Ⓒ Ⓓ	4	Ⓐ Ⓑ Ⓒ	8	Ⓐ Ⓑ Ⓒ Ⓓ	11	Ⓐ Ⓑ Ⓒ Ⓓ
		5	Ⓐ Ⓑ Ⓒ	9	Ⓐ Ⓑ Ⓒ Ⓓ	12	Ⓐ Ⓑ Ⓒ Ⓓ
		6	Ⓐ Ⓑ Ⓒ				

SHOOT UP TO THE TOEIC® TEST LISTENING

Unit 18 Answer Sheet No. ______ Name ______

Part 1		Part 2		Part 3		Part 4	
1	Ⓐ Ⓑ Ⓒ Ⓓ	3	Ⓐ Ⓑ Ⓒ	7	Ⓐ Ⓑ Ⓒ Ⓓ	10	Ⓐ Ⓑ Ⓒ Ⓓ
2	Ⓐ Ⓑ Ⓒ Ⓓ	4	Ⓐ Ⓑ Ⓒ	8	Ⓐ Ⓑ Ⓒ Ⓓ	11	Ⓐ Ⓑ Ⓒ Ⓓ
		5	Ⓐ Ⓑ Ⓒ	9	Ⓐ Ⓑ Ⓒ Ⓓ	12	Ⓐ Ⓑ Ⓒ Ⓓ
		6	Ⓐ Ⓑ Ⓒ				

SHOOT UP TO THE TOEIC® TEST LISTENING

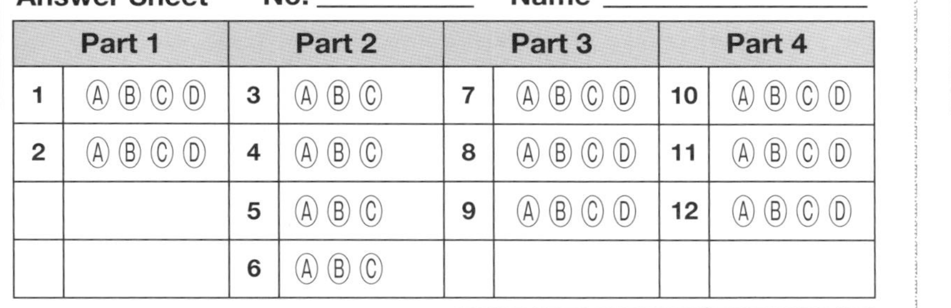

Unit 19 Answer Sheet No. ________ Name ______________

Part 1		Part 2		Part 3		Part 4	
1	Ⓐ Ⓑ Ⓒ Ⓓ	3	Ⓐ Ⓑ Ⓒ	7	Ⓐ Ⓑ Ⓒ Ⓓ	10	Ⓐ Ⓑ Ⓒ Ⓓ
2	Ⓐ Ⓑ Ⓒ Ⓓ	4	Ⓐ Ⓑ Ⓒ	8	Ⓐ Ⓑ Ⓒ Ⓓ	11	Ⓐ Ⓑ Ⓒ Ⓓ
		5	Ⓐ Ⓑ Ⓒ	9	Ⓐ Ⓑ Ⓒ Ⓓ	12	Ⓐ Ⓑ Ⓒ Ⓓ
		6	Ⓐ Ⓑ Ⓒ				

SHOOT UP TO THE TOEIC® TEST LISTENING

Unit 20 Answer Sheet No. ________ Name ______________

Part 1		Part 2		Part 3		Part 4	
1	Ⓐ Ⓑ Ⓒ Ⓓ	3	Ⓐ Ⓑ Ⓒ	7	Ⓐ Ⓑ Ⓒ Ⓓ	10	Ⓐ Ⓑ Ⓒ Ⓓ
2	Ⓐ Ⓑ Ⓒ Ⓓ	4	Ⓐ Ⓑ Ⓒ	8	Ⓐ Ⓑ Ⓒ Ⓓ	11	Ⓐ Ⓑ Ⓒ Ⓓ
		5	Ⓐ Ⓑ Ⓒ	9	Ⓐ Ⓑ Ⓒ Ⓓ	12	Ⓐ Ⓑ Ⓒ Ⓓ
		6	Ⓐ Ⓑ Ⓒ				

SHOOT UP TO THE TOEIC® TEST LISTENING

Unit 21 Answer Sheet No. ________ Name ______________

Part 1		Part 2		Part 3		Part 4	
1	Ⓐ Ⓑ Ⓒ Ⓓ	3	Ⓐ Ⓑ Ⓒ	7	Ⓐ Ⓑ Ⓒ Ⓓ	10	Ⓐ Ⓑ Ⓒ Ⓓ
2	Ⓐ Ⓑ Ⓒ Ⓓ	4	Ⓐ Ⓑ Ⓒ	8	Ⓐ Ⓑ Ⓒ Ⓓ	11	Ⓐ Ⓑ Ⓒ Ⓓ
		5	Ⓐ Ⓑ Ⓒ	9	Ⓐ Ⓑ Ⓒ Ⓓ	12	Ⓐ Ⓑ Ⓒ Ⓓ
		6	Ⓐ Ⓑ Ⓒ				

SHOOT UP TO THE TOEIC® TEST LISTENING

Unit 22 Answer Sheet No. ________ Name ______________

Part 1		Part 2		Part 3		Part 4	
1	Ⓐ Ⓑ Ⓒ Ⓓ	3	Ⓐ Ⓑ Ⓒ	7	Ⓐ Ⓑ Ⓒ Ⓓ	10	Ⓐ Ⓑ Ⓒ Ⓓ
2	Ⓐ Ⓑ Ⓒ Ⓓ	4	Ⓐ Ⓑ Ⓒ	8	Ⓐ Ⓑ Ⓒ Ⓓ	11	Ⓐ Ⓑ Ⓒ Ⓓ
		5	Ⓐ Ⓑ Ⓒ	9	Ⓐ Ⓑ Ⓒ Ⓓ	12	Ⓐ Ⓑ Ⓒ Ⓓ
		6	Ⓐ Ⓑ Ⓒ				

SHOOT UP TO THE TOEIC® TEST LISTENING

Unit 23 Answer Sheet No. ________ Name ______________

Part 1		Part 2		Part 3		Part 4	
1	Ⓐ Ⓑ Ⓒ Ⓓ	3	Ⓐ Ⓑ Ⓒ	7	Ⓐ Ⓑ Ⓒ Ⓓ	10	Ⓐ Ⓑ Ⓒ Ⓓ
2	Ⓐ Ⓑ Ⓒ Ⓓ	4	Ⓐ Ⓑ Ⓒ	8	Ⓐ Ⓑ Ⓒ Ⓓ	11	Ⓐ Ⓑ Ⓒ Ⓓ
		5	Ⓐ Ⓑ Ⓒ	9	Ⓐ Ⓑ Ⓒ Ⓓ	12	Ⓐ Ⓑ Ⓒ Ⓓ
		6	Ⓐ Ⓑ Ⓒ				

SHOOT UP TO THE TOEIC® TEST LISTENING

Unit 24 Answer Sheet No. ________ Name ______________

Part 1		Part 2		Part 3		Part 4	
1	Ⓐ Ⓑ Ⓒ Ⓓ	3	Ⓐ Ⓑ Ⓒ	7	Ⓐ Ⓑ Ⓒ Ⓓ	10	Ⓐ Ⓑ Ⓒ Ⓓ
2	Ⓐ Ⓑ Ⓒ Ⓓ	4	Ⓐ Ⓑ Ⓒ	8	Ⓐ Ⓑ Ⓒ Ⓓ	11	Ⓐ Ⓑ Ⓒ Ⓓ
		5	Ⓐ Ⓑ Ⓒ	9	Ⓐ Ⓑ Ⓒ Ⓓ	12	Ⓐ Ⓑ Ⓒ Ⓓ
		6	Ⓐ Ⓑ Ⓒ				

SHOOT UP TO THE TOEIC® TEST LISTENING